NEW JERSEY'S

TROLLEY HERITAGE

Atlantic City & Shore Railroad car No. 106 is heading a two-car train on Atlantic Avenue on a trip to Ocean City on August 31, 1941. This was one of twenty cars (Nos. 101–120) built in 1905 by the John Stephenson Company of Elizabeth, New Jersey. The company was acquired by the J. G. Brill Company in 1904; however, it continued to operate under the Stephenson name until 1917 when the plant was sold to Standard Aero Corporation for the production of airplanes. (*F. J. Goldsmith Jr. photograph, Joseph P. Saitta curator, Craig Knox collection*)

In 1946, an Atlantic City & Shore Railroad trolley car, built by the John Stephenson Company in 1905, is on the Great Egg Harbor trestle at Somers Point, New Jersey. (*Craig Knox collection*)

NEW JERSEY'S
TROLLEY HERITAGE

KENNETH C. SPRINGIRTH

AMERICA
THROUGH TIME®
ADDING COLOR TO AMERICAN HISTORY

On December 28, 1955, Atlantic City Transportation Company (ACTC) Brilliner No. 222 (originally No. 6922), one of twenty-five cars (originally Nos. 6901–6925, later renumbered 201–225) built between 1938 and 1940 by J. G. Brill Company, is at Longport waiting for departure time for its next trip to the Inlet in Atlantic City. (*Bob's Photos collection*)

On top portion of cover: Atlantic City & Shore Railroad car No. 113 is at the Virginia Avenue Terminal in Atlantic City with special on the destination sign. Between Atlantic City and Somers Point, trolleys shared trackage with the West Jersey & Seashore Railroad (WJ&S), controlled by the Pennsylvania Railroad, using the third rail between Atlantic City and Pleasantville, which was once used by the WJ&S Camden to Atlantic City wooden MU cars. After the September 11, 1946 trestle fire that destroyed a portion of the bridge between Somers Point and Ocean City, buses took over the Somers Point to Ocean City section. Trolleys continued to provide service between Atlantic City and Somers Point until service ended on January 18, 1948. (*Craig Knox collection*)

On bottom portion of cover: Atlantic City Transportation Company (ACTC) car No. 6890 is on picturesque Atlantic Avenue in local service on the Atlantic City to Longport line. This double-truck, double-ended, thirteen-passenger window car was built by J. G. Brill Company in 1923. (*Craig Knox collection*)

Back Cover: Longport Loop is the location of ACTC car No. 207 (originally No. 6907) waiting for departure time in December 1955. This was one of twenty-five "Brilliners" built for local service between Atlantic City and Longport. Owned by the Pennsylvania Railroad, which controlled the WJ&S, it was operated by the Atlantic City & Shore Railroad until it was sold to the Atlantic City Transportation Company in 1945. (*Bob's Photos collection*)

America Through Time is an imprint of Fonthill Media LLC
www.through-time.com | office@through-time.com

First published 2020

ISBN 978-1-63499-224-4

Typeset in Utopia Std
Printed and bound in England

Published by Arcadia Publishing by arrangement with Fonthill Media LLC
For all general information, please contact Arcadia Publishing:

Telephone: 843-853-2070
Fax: 843-853-0044
E-mail: sales@arcadiapublishing.com
For customer service and orders:
Toll-Free 1-888-313-2665

www.arcadiapublishing.com

Contents

	Acknowledgments	6
	Introduction	7
1	Shore Fast Line	13
2	Atlantic City Trolley Cars	37
3	Five Mile Beach Electric Railway	67
4	Pennsylvania–Reading Seashore Lines	73
5	Route 7 City Subway in Newark	79
6	Hudson-Bergen Light Rail Line	113
7	River Line	119

Acknowledgments

This book is dedicated to my long-time friend Craig Knox whose lifelong effort to preserve New Jersey trolley car photos contributed to a significant number of the images used in this book. We both graduated from Lansdowne Aldan High School in Lansdowne, Pennsylvania. Pictures came from many sources, including Richard Allman, John Brinckmann, Bob's Photos, Mervin E. Borgnis, David H. Cope, Peter D. Ehrlich, Joseph F. Eid, Jr., Bob Foley, F. J. Goldsmith, Jr., Charlie Houser, Sr., Krambles-Peterson archives, Robert G. Lewis, R. L. Long, H. Gerald Mac Donald Graphic Arts, M. D. Mc Carter, S. D. Maguire, Bill Milow, E. Lewis Pardee, John A. Rehor, Lee Rogers, Joseph P. Saitta, Clifford R. Scholes, Senior Studios, Richard S. Short, Harold A. Smith, Robert J. Wasche, Don Wentzel, and Craig Knox. Sources of information included *Atlantic City's Interurban Trolley Systems* by Anthony Marino in the Atlantic County Historical Society 2014 Sixty-Seventh Yearbook Volume 17 Number 3 Pages 30–40; *Headlights*, various issues published by the Electric Railroaders' Association; *Hudson-Bergen Light Rail* by Alfred E. Fazio, P.E.; *Pennsylvania-Reading Seashore Lines* by Frederick A. Kramer; *River Line, Southern New Jersey's New Interurban Railway* by Alfred E. Fazio, P.E.; *Streetcars of New Jersey* by Joseph F. Eid, Jr., and Barker Gummere; *The Newark City Subway Lines* by John Harrington Riley; *The Public Service Trolley Lines in New Jersey* by Edward Hamm, Jr.; *Tramways & Urban Transit*, October 2001, Page 386.

Well maintained New Jersey Transit car No. 12 is loading passengers at the Route 7 Franklin Avenue terminus of the Newark City Subway on July 8, 1997. This was originally car No. 326, one of twenty cars (Nos. 320–339) delivered during December 1946 to January 1947 by St. Louis Car Company for Twin City Rapid Transit Company of Minneapolis/St. Paul, Minnesota. Weighing 37,000 pounds and seating fifty-two, each car was powered by four General Electric type 1220 motors. (*Kenneth C. Springirth photograph*)

Introduction

The Camden and Atlantic Railroad (C&A) was completed to Atlantic City with regular passenger service beginning July 1, 1854. With the C&A delivering passengers to this growing city, a C&A conductor had the idea of building the Atlantic City Boardwalk to keep sand out of C&A passenger cars. Opened on June 16, 1870, the 10-foot-wide boardwalk was built at a cost of $5,000. On May 10, 1889, electric trolley cars began operating, and the line was completed on June 15, 1893 from the Inlet at the north end of Atlantic City primarily on Atlantic Avenue via Ventnor and Margate to Longport. Trolley car service increased to handle the crowds attracted to Atlantic City viewing the shows, big band music of the era, the Miss America pageant, and various parades. With the beginning of jitney operation in 1915 followed by more people buying automobiles, ridership began to decline. A demonstrator Brilliner trolley car was purchased in 1938 followed by twenty-four more in 1940 from J. G. Brill Company. These distinctive cream and black trolley cars became known as the "Miss America Fleet." During World War II, Convention Hall on the Boardwalk became a military training facility. Armed forces personnel marched on the Boardwalk. The Atlantic City Transportation Company purchased the Atlantic City–Longport trolley car line in 1945 and Atlantic City & Shore Railroad in 1946. Atlantic City–Longport trolley car service ended on December 28, 1955, leaving Newark as the only trolley car line remaining in New Jersey.

The Five Mile Beach Electric Railway began full revenue service on June 11, 1903. Operating New Jersey's last open trolley cars, service ended at the close of 1945 summer season. Steam railroad passenger service connecting Pleasantville to Somers Point began in 1881 by the Pleasantville & Ocean City Railroad. At Somers Point, passengers travelled by steamboat to Ocean City. In 1884, it merged into the West Jersey & Seashore division of the Pennsylvania Railroad. The Atlantic & Suburban Traction Company (A&S) began service in 1903 from the Boardwalk at Florida Avenue in Atlantic City to Pleasantville. Service was extended to Somers Point. On March 31, 1929, the A&S was abandoned.

In 1906, the Shore Fast Line began operation connecting Atlantic City with Somers Point and was opened to Ocean City in 1907. After the September 11, 1946 fire destroyed the bridge between Somers Point and Ocean City, buses took over the Somers Point to Ocean City section. Trolley car service between Atlantic City and Somers Point ended on January 18, 1948.

In Newark, with the conversion of Route 21 (Orange Street) and Route 29 (Bloomfield) to bus operation on March 30, 1952, Route 7 (City Subway), which opened on May 26, 1935, was the only remaining trolley car line in the city of Newark. Public Service Coordinated Transport (PSCT) purchased thirty used Presidents' Conference Committee (PCC) cars from Twin Cities Rapid Transit Company of Minneapolis–St. Paul. By the end of January 1954, PCC cars had replaced all of the older cars. The vintage, well-maintained Presidents' Conference Committee (PCC) cars were replaced by new light rail vehicles built by Kinkisharyo in September 2001. Route 7 was extended from its Franklin Avenue terminus to Grove Street in Bloomfield on June 22, 2002.

New Jersey Transit's Hudson-Bergen Light Rail Line (HBLR), New Jersey's first new light rail line, opened on April 15, 2000 from 34th Street in Bayonne to Exchange Place in Jersey City with a branch line to West Side Avenue. New light rail vehicles almost identical to those for the Newark City Subway line were placed in service. The line was opened to Hoboken Terminal on September 29, 2002. As a result of completing several extensions, the HBLR is 17 miles long and has become part of New Jersey's smart growth strategy to reduce automobile ridership and revitalize older urban and suburban areas through transit-oriented development. In the *Forbes* August 1, 2011 issue titled "America's Top Transportation Cities," the City of Hoboken in Hudson County, New Jersey, has 56 percent of working residents using public transit for commuting purposes, which is the highest in the U.S. New York City is second with an estimated 54.7 percent of its workers using public transit. Hoboken's population declined from 70,324 in 1910 to 33,397 in 1990 and increased to 38,577 in 2000 and 50,005 in 2010. Bayonne's population declined from 88,979 in 1930 to 61,444 in 1990 and increased to 61,842 in 2000 and 63,024 in 2010. In both cities, the rail line is a positive factor in attracting residents.

New Jersey Transit opened the 34-mile, diesel-powered River Line connecting Camden and Trenton on March 14, 2004. With several blocks of street running in Camden, for the purposes of this book, this line will be classified as a trolley line.

In this 1908 postcard, the Orange Mountain Railway (OMR) trolley is from Eagle Rock. OMR, chartered on July 16, 1906, leased the Orange Mountain Traction Company and constructed a new right of way with easier grades up the mountain. Opening in 1908, the line operated every thirty minutes. It was losing money and never paid a dividend. When the company failed to pay its electric bill, its power was shut off and service ended on June 14, 1914.

Two Atlantic Coast Electric Railway Company (ACER) cars are passing Railroad Square in the city of Asbury Park, Monmouth County, New Jersey, in this postcard view around 1910. The line operated ninety-four cars on its 36-mile system that connected Long Branch via Asbury Park with Sea Girt. In 1924, ACER was merged into the Coast Cities Railway. Its last trolley line, Belmar, ended service on October 22, 1931.

The Broad Street bridge in Bridgeton, Cumberland County, New Jersey, is the location of two single-truck Bridgeton & Millville Traction Company trolley cars around 1911. Regular service between Bridgeton and Millville began on August 12, 1893. In 1918, the line operated twenty-nine cars on 37.87 miles of track. Ridership declined as automobile ownership increased. Operation ended at midnight on June 15, 1922.

Two New Jersey Traction Company (NJTC) trolley cars are passing on Main Street near Greenwood Avenue in East Orange, Essex County, New Jersey, in 1910 postcard. The NJTC electrified the line between the Pennsylvania Railroad Station in Newark to the Roseville Car House on Main Street in East Orange.

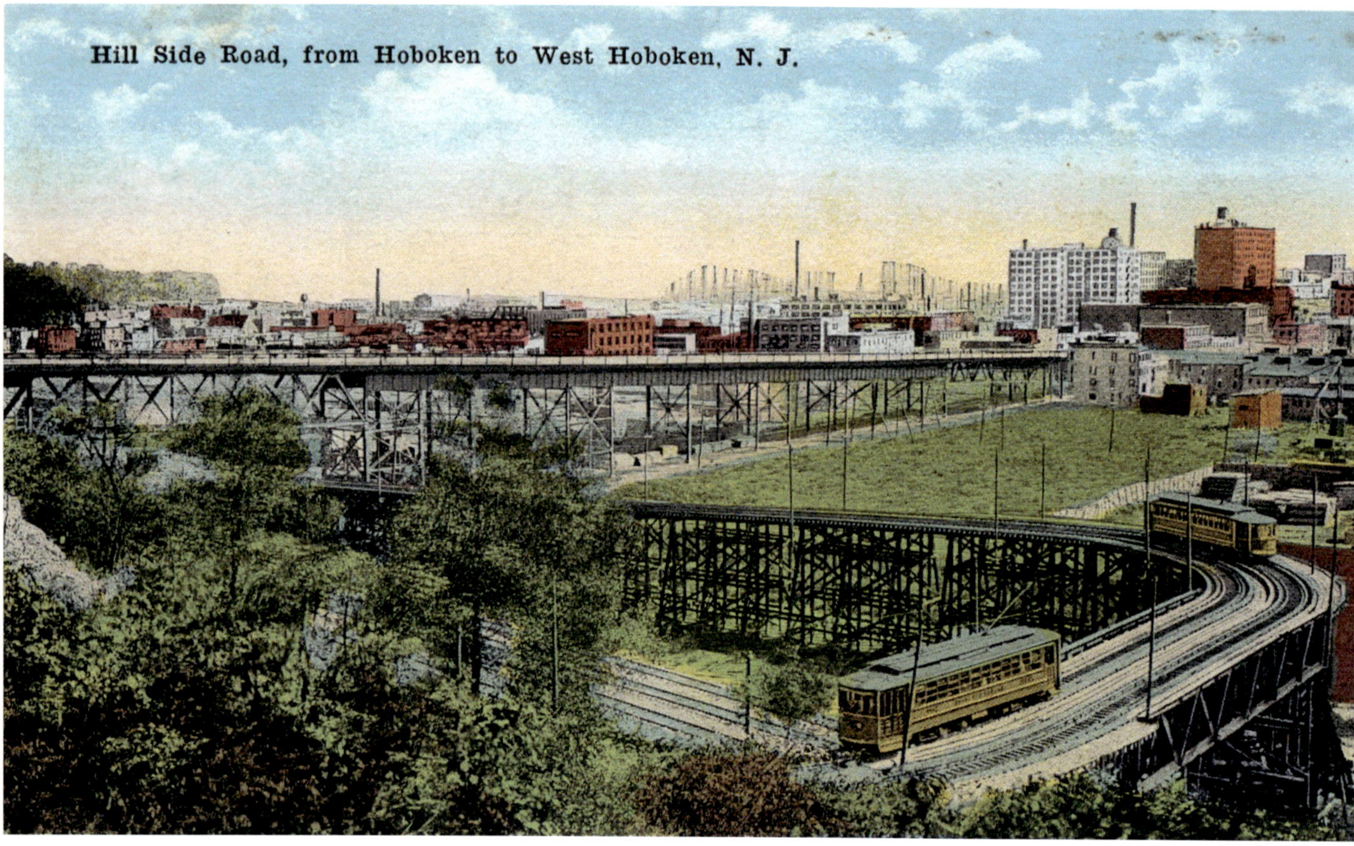

Above: In this 1912 postcard view, two Public Service Railway Company (PSRC) trolley cars are on the Hill Side Road bridge traveling from Hoboken to West Hoboken, Hudson County, New Jersey. PSRC grew from 675 miles of track in 1911 to 891 miles of track by 1918. In 1915, PSRC carried 414 million riders and, with pride, noted: "Not one passenger was killed in all of those miles."

Left: Broad Street at Market Street in Newark, New Jersey, had a busy flow of trolley cars and pedestrian traffic in this 1912 postcard scene. Frequency of service at this intersection increased 35.7 percent from 387 cars per hour in 1905 to 525 cars per hour in 1910. The Broad Street line was electrified by the New Jersey Traction Company in 1892, leased to the Consolidated Traction Company on January 2, 1894, and was merged into the Public Service Railway Company on August 20, 1907.

Newark, the largest city in New Jersey, also had the most comprehensive trolley system in the state. Trolley car service was excellent, and downtown Newark was busy as evidenced by this 1912 postcard scene on Market Street west of Broad Street at noon in Newark.

In this 1914 postcard, two Public Service Railway Company trolley cars are on Market Street at the Pennsylvania Railroad station in Newark. In 1919, service frequency on the Market Street Line was three minutes and thirty seconds in the morning rush hour, six minutes mid-morning, five minutes early afternoon, and three minutes in the afternoon rush hour.

Two Trenton Street Railway trolley cars are passing on Broad Street at Hanover in this 1910 postcard view. The Trenton & Mercer County Traction Corp. (TMCTC), chartered on October 5, 1910, leased the Trenton Street Railway. On November 23, 1929, TMCTC merged into the Trenton Transit Company. By December 9, 1934, the remaining trolley lines were converted to bus operation.

Atlantic City & Shore Railroad car No. 113 is in Ocean City waiting for departure time in 1946. The orange with cream front bowtie gave this car a distinctive look. Primary purpose of the 16.2-mile line connecting Ocean City with Atlantic City was to carry passengers; however, it also carried baggage and mail. (*Robert J. Wasche photograph, Craig Knox collection*)

1

Shore Fast Line

Chartered on October 21, 1905, the Atlantic City & Shore Railroad (ACSR) was chartered to build an electric line between Atlantic City and Ocean City. The company used Central Passenger Railway tracks west from the Boardwalk to Adriatic Avenue via Virginia Avenue. At which point, the ACSR built a double-track line. The line entered the central strip of Absecon Boulevard, made a left on to Marmora Avenue, and entered private right of way to the Thorofare drawbridge. Overhead wire was used for the line from the Boardwalk to the drawbridge. At which point, the third rail was used as the line crossed the Thorofare drawbridge and then on a curved trestle that spanned the West Jersey & Seashore Railroad (steam), Reading Railroad, and the West Jersey & Seashore Railroad (electric). It descended to the West Jersey & Seashore Railroad tracks joining them at Meadows Tower. The double-track line to Pleasantville used the third rail West Jersey & Seashore Railroad. At Pleasantville, the line used the Somers Point branch of the West Jersey & Seashore Railroad to Egg Harbor Bay and installed overhead wire. A substation was built at Somers Point. Service began on August 25, 1906 with fifteen-minute headway between Atlantic City and Pleasantville and hourly service to Somers Point. On March 19, 1906, the Atlantic City & Ocean City Railroad was chartered and extended the ACSR line from Somers Point across Egg Harbor Bay eastward to Bay Avenue and Eighth Street in Ocean City. Service began July 4, 1907, and in 1908, the line was extended east to the Boardwalk.

On July 14, 1935, the route changed to leave the Virginia Avenue terminal turning left on to Atlantic Avenue and right on to Mississippi Avenue. The line joined the West Jersey line east of the Thorofare drawbridge. After the September 11, 1946 fire destroyed part of the Great Egg Harbor Bay trestle, buses operated between Ocean City and Somers Point. On January 18, 1948, the Atlantic City & Shore Railroad ended electric passenger service between Atlantic City and Somers Point.

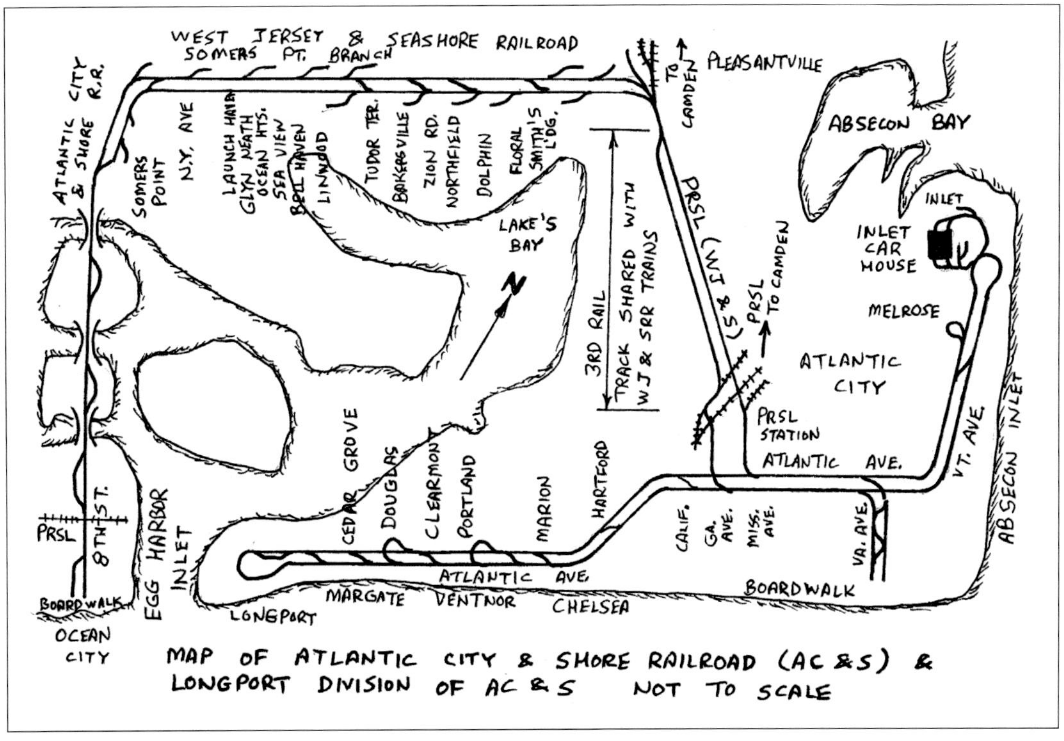

This map shows the Atlantic City & Shore Railroad (ACSR), also known as the Shore Fast Line, from Atlantic City via Somers Point to Ocean City, plus the ACSR Atlantic Avenue & Longport Division local trolley car service that operated from Atlantic City to Longport.

ACSR car No. 110 is shown in this 1910 postcard view. The line used the third rail between Atlantic City and Pleasantville (both cities are in Atlantic County, New Jersey) over which the Camden to Atlantic City wooden multiple unit cars of the West Jersey & Seashore Railroad (WJ&S) once ran. (*Craig Knox collection*)

In this 1948 view, ACSR wooden interurban car No. 115 is at Pleasantville (named for its surroundings). The John Stephenson Company, which built twenty of these cars (Nos. 101–120) in 1905, was acquired by J. G. Brill Company in 1904. It was licensed to build Brill cars; however, it was never equipped with the machinery to manufacture steel cars. (*Lee Rogers photograph, Craig Knox collection*)

In the 1940s, double-truck, double-end ACSR cars No. 112 and 104 are at the Virginia Avenue and Boardwalk terminal in Atlantic City. To compete with the automobile in 1936, the line using an airline approach added a trolley hostess on the car to assist passengers, provide newspapers plus magazines, and information to passengers. (*Craig Knox collection*)

ACSR car No. 106 is heading a two-car train on Atlantic Avenue in Atlantic City in August 1944. Twenty (45.415-foot-long by 8.8-foot-wide body) cars (Nos. 101–120) were built by the John Stephenson Company in 1905 for the ACSR of which seventeen cars (Nos. 101–117) were passenger cars seating fifty-two passengers. Cars Nos. 118 and 119 were combination cars; however, later, car No. 118 was rebuilt into a passenger car while car No. 120 was a funeral car and was later rebuilt into a parlor car. (*Craig Knox collection*)

In the mid-1940s, ACSR car No. 115 is on Atlantic Avenue in downtown Atlantic City. The company's slogan was "See All and Do All by the Shore Fast Line." While ACSR offered a 75-cent round-trip fare between Atlantic City and Ocean City, they also encouraged Atlantic City residents to use the Atlantic Avenue trolley to Longport, take a boat to Ocean City, and return by the Shore Fast Line. (*Charlie Houser Sr. photograph, Craig Knox collection*)

ACSR car No. 108 is at the Virginia Avenue terminus in Atlantic City along with two other trolley cars around 1945. (*Charlie Houser Sr. photograph, Craig Knox collection*)

Passing vintage automobiles of the 1940s, an ACSR two-car train headed by car No. 106 is on Atlantic Avenue in Atlantic City. Company employees cared about their customers. A family might receive a phone call from a conductor stating, "Would you please meet trolley 'No.' at 'Location' at 'time' as it is felt that the passenger should be escorted home." It might have been for medical reasons or simply reaction to a certain drink. (*Craig Knox collection*)

With both poles down, well-dressed passengers are exiting ACSR car No. 113 at the 8th Street and Boardwalk terminus in Ocean City, a city in Cape May County, New Jersey. The back pole will soon be lifted to the wire for the return trip to Atlantic City in 1945. (*Krambles-Peterson archives, Craig Knox collection*)

In the late afternoon of 1946, ACSR car No. 105 is on 8th Street at Central Avenue in Ocean City. Even though the twenty-car fleet was built by one company, there were operational differences between cars, and over a period of time, motormen became skilled in handling those individual car characteristics. (*Craig Knox collection*)

ACSR car No. 105 is at the Atlantic City meadows around 1945. The last car at night would stop at each station and turn off the station lights. In addition, any disabled car would be taken back to the car barn. (*Craig Knox collection*)

On June 15, 1947, ACSR car No. 104 is on the Somers Point trestle for a photo stop on a National Railway Historical Society charter trip. (*John Brinckmann photograph, Craig Knox collection*)

Around 1938, an ACSR car is heading for Ocean City. (*David H. Cope photograph, Richard Allman curator, Craig Knox collection*)

ACSR interurban car No. 117 is on a layover on the Great Egg Harbor trestle at Somers Point on October 11, 1947 for the return trip to Atlantic City. The September 11, 1946 fire destroyed part of the Great Egg Harbor Bay trestle, and buses operated between Ocean City and Somers Point. (*John A. Rehor photograph, Craig Knox collection*)

In 1940, ACSR car No. 104 is entering Atlantic City. Note the difference in the height of the retriever (black circular object on front and rear of the car that brings back the wire from the trolley pole) as seen on car No. 104 in the cream color portion of the triangle compared to the position of the retriever on cars 105 and 113 on the border of the cream and orange-colored triangles on the picture on the bottom of page 21. That difference in height from ground level occurred because of the height of the shop employee making the installation. (*David H. Cope photograph, Craig Knox collection*)

Ocean City is the destination for ACSR car No. 101 at Pleasantville around 1938. This was a junction point for the West Jersey & Seashore Railroad to Camden. (*David H. Cope photograph, Richard Allman curator, Craig Knox collection*)

On January 11, 1948, ACSR cars Nos. 105 and 113 are at Somers Point, a city in Atlantic County, New Jersey. (*Clifford R. Scholes photograph, Craig Knox collection*)

Virginia Avenue at the Boardwalk in Atlantic City is the location of ACSR car No. 108 around 1940. The sign on the left of the picture advertises "Fast Line to Ocean City." The October 1, 1933 to March 31, 1934 timetable showed a fifty-two-minute travel time by trolley car between Atlantic City and Ocean City. In later years, the schedule was slower to keep the aging cars in service. (*Craig Knox collection*)

ACSR car No. 108 is on the Pennsylvania-Reading Seashore Line between Pleasantville and Atlantic City in the mid-1940s. (*E. Lewis Pardee photograph, Craig Knox collection*)

In 1941, ACSR cars Nos. 110 and 104 are operating in a two-car train on Atlantic Avenue in Atlantic City. (*Krambles-Peterson archives, Craig Knox collection*)

The Virginia Avenue and Boardwalk terminus in Atlantic City is the location of ACSR car No. 116 around 1945. Note the number box on the roof of the car. The illuminated number box on the car roof provided twenty-four-hour car identification to the Pennsylvania Railroad tower man at Pleasantville and the tower man at Meadows to record the passage of each car. In 1924, car No. 116 was featured at the American Electric Railway Convention to show how an older car could be remodeled. (*Craig Knox collection*)

In 1947, ACSR car No. 102 is on Virginia Avenue in Atlantic City heading for Ocean City. (*David H. Cope photograph, Richard Allman curator, Craig Knox collection*)

The Virginia Avenue and Boardwalk terminal in Atlantic City is the location of four ACSR cars, of which Nos. 111 and 113 are in clear view, in the mid-1940s. When the passenger count reached thirty-seven, a second car was added. The company attempted to enhance the comfort of passengers by limiting the number of standees within reason. (*Craig Knox collection*)

In 1938, ACSR car No. 106 is on Virginia Avenue in Atlantic City. Note the well-dressed pedestrians on the sidewalk. (*Clifford R. Scholes photograph, Craig Knox collection*)

ACSR car No. 104 is handling a short-turn trip from Atlantic City to Somers Point in 1945. (*John A. Rehor photograph, Craig Knox collection*)

Traveling north on Virginia Avenue in 1947, ACSR car No. 101 is a short distance from Atlantic Avenue where it will make a left turn and use Longport Division trackage followed by a right turn on to Pennsylvania-Reading Seashore Line trackage, followed by a left turn onto West Jersey & Seashore Railroad trackage to Linwood, a cut back on the line to Ocean City. (*David H. Cope photograph, Richard Allman curator, Craig Knox collection*)

In 1947, ACSR car No. 101 is turning from Virginia Avenue on to Atlantic Avenue in Atlantic City in 1947 for a trip to Linwood, a cut back on the line to Ocean City. (*David H. Cope photograph, Richard Allman curator, Craig Knox collection*)

Virginia Avenue at Pacific Avenue in Atlantic City is the location of ACSR car No. 110 around 1945. (*Craig Knox collection*)

On January 17, 1948, ACSR car No. 113 is at the Pleasantville station. Pleasantville was once a major junction where passengers from electric trains heading to Atlantic City would board at Pleasantville for Ocean City. (*Mervin E. Borgnis photograph, Craig Knox collection*)

ACSR car No. 114 is at Pleasantville heading left at the junction on the Ocean City line for a short-turn trip to Linwood, a city in Atlantic County nine miles west of Atlantic City primarily a residential community with a significant portion of its population employed in professional services and executive positions. (*David H. Cope photograph, Richard Allman curator, Craig Knox collection*)

In 1947, ACSR car No. 115 is at Somers Point, which is about 10 miles southwest of Atlantic City. This is the oldest settlement in Atlantic County, New Jersey. (*Mervin E. Borgnis photograph, Craig Knox collection*)

ACSR car No. 117 is at the 8th Street and Boardwalk terminal in Ocean City on August 2, 1940. (*Bob Foley photograph, Craig Knox collection*)

The Ocean City terminal is the location of ACSR car No. 101 in 1939. (*David H. Cope photograph, Richard Allman curator, Craig Knox collection*)

In May 1944, ACSR car No. 105 is at the Ocean City terminus. (*Krambles-Peterson archives, Craig Knox collection*)

From left to right in 1943: ACSR car No. 110 is on the siding and car No. 114 is at the Linwood, New Jersey, station for a return trip to Boardwalk and Virginia Avenue in Atlantic City. (*David H. Cope photograph, Richard Allman curator, Craig Knox collection*)

A two-car ACSR train is proceeding on Virginia Avenue and one car is at the Boardwalk terminal in 1947 in this overhead view at Atlantic City. (*David H. Cope photograph, Craig Knox collection*)

In 1947, ACSR car No. 109 is at Somers Point. The power house and station are in front of the legendary Tony Mart nightclub that operated from the summer of 1945 to its last day on September 14, 1982 with recording stars, plus rock and roll bands, on two stages and two dance floors. (*Richard S. Short photograph, Craig Knox collection*)

Well-dressed passengers are waiting at the Pleasantville shelter for the two-car ACSR train to come to a stop in the mid-1940s. (*Robert G. Lewis photograph, Craig Knox collection*)

ACSR car No. 111 is at the Pleasantville station on its 1946 trip to Atlantic City. (*M.D. McCarter photograph, Craig Knox collection*)

Poles are down as a two-car ACSR train passes through Pleasantville powered by the visible third rail in 1940. The ACSR used the WJ&S's third rail line from just outside of Atlantic City to Pleasantville. At Pleasantville, the ACSR switched over to the WJ&S branch line to Somers Point where that leased trackage was electrified with overhead wire. (*Robert G. Lewis photograph, Craig Knox collection*)

A two-car train composed of two ACSR cars. Nos. 108 and 118 are on Atlantic Avenue in Atlantic City in September 1946. (*John Brinckmann photograph, Craig Knox collection*)

Passengers are boarding ACSR car No. 105 at Pleasantville in 1945. (*Clifford R. Scholes photograph, Craig Knox collection*)

On a winter day in 1945, ACSR car No. 115 is pushing through the melting snow on Atlantic Avenue in Atlantic City. Motormen liked this car because of its speed and dependability; however, conductors disliked the difficulty of ringing up a fare on the car's fare register. (*M.D. McCarter photograph, Craig Knox collection*)

ACSR car No. 114 is at the New York Avenue Station in Somers Point in 1945. (*Senior Studios photograph, Craig Knox collection*)

On July 21, 1940, ACSR cars Nos. 102 and 110 are passing on what is probably a rail excursion photo stop in the causeway between Somers Point and Ocean City. (*Clifford R. Scholes photograph, Craig Knox collection*)

On January 18, 1948, the last day of scheduled service, ACSR car No. 113 is eastbound on Virginia Avenue heading for the Boardwalk terminus in Atlantic City. (*John A. Rehor photograph, Craig Knox collection*)

In Atlantic City on the last day of scheduled service, January 18, 1948, ACSR car No. 105 has hand painted letters "Last Car-Rest in Peace" on the side of the car and on the front of the car below the window, "I made it! Next stop scrap pile." On June 22, 2019, New Jersey Transit operates two daily bus routes between Atlantic City and Ocean City. Route 507 uses Shore Road between the Pleasantville Bus Terminal and Highway 52 in Somers Point with a frequency that varies from twenty minutes to hourly depending on the time of day, while Route 509 generally has an hourly frequency and uses New Road (Highway 9) with only seven trips operating beyond Somers Point to Ocean City. (*Richard S. Short photograph, Craig Knox collection*)

2

Atlantic City Trolley Cars

The Camden & Atlantic Railroad (C&A) completed a standard-gauge steam railroad from Camden to Atlantic City with train service beginning July 1, 1854. Entering Atlantic City, the line turned on to Atlantic Avenue and ended at the Inlet. While the trains made several stops on Atlantic Avenue, the newly built homes and hotels needed more frequent service. The C&A established its own horse-car line in 1875, which used the railroad's tracks from South Carolina Avenue on Atlantic Avenue to the Inlet. This was extended south on Atlantic Avenue to Florida Avenue in 1877, extended south to Margate in 1881, and extended again to Longport. The line was converted to electric operation with the first car tested on April 24, 1889, regular service began on May 10, 1889, and line completed to Longport on June 15, 1893. Both open and enclosed cars were used on the Atlantic City to Longport trolley line. The Pennsylvania Railroad acquired the C&A in 1893 and was merged in 1896 into the West Jersey & Seashore Railroad. During 1905-1906, the line from Camden via Newfield to Atlantic City was electrified.

During World War I, Philadelphia Rapid Transit Company had a need for additional cars to serve the 30,000 workers at the Hog Island Shipyard on the Delaware River near Philadelphia. The Emergency Fleet Corporation (EFC) had the J. G. Brill Company build 100 of these "Hog Island cars" (Nos. 4000–4099) and the U.S. Housing Corporation had thirty cars (Nos. 4100–4129) built by J. G. Brill Company. Since the Atlantic Avenue to Longport line was owned by the Pennsylvania Railroad, the twelve Hog Island cars purchased for this line after World War I was over were renumbered 6845–6850 and 6885–6890 to fit into the railroad's numbering system.

On September 27, 1931, electric service was discontinued between Camden and Atlantic City. Electric rail service continued between Camden and Millville until it was discontinued on September 8, 1949. Open cars were used in daily summer service during the summer of 1936. In the summers of 1937 and 1938, open cars were only used when there was heavy passenger traffic. Open cars made their last runs on July 4, 1939 and were scrapped at the end of the summer of 1939. The Atlantic Avenue & Longport Division modernized their car fleet. Although the J. G. Brill Company never built Presidents' Conference Committee cars, it designed a streamlined trolley car known as a Brilliner with a riveted steel body design. In 1938, Brilliner trolley car No. 6891 was received as a demonstrator. It was renumbered 6901 in 1940 and renumbered again as 201 in 1945. By September 2, 1940, a total of twenty-five Brilliners (numbered 6901–6925) were built for Atlantic City. These cars covered the base service. Known as the "Miss America Fleet," they were renumbered 201–225 in 1945. The twelve older "Hog Island" cars were used during peak periods. The only other Brilliners built were three for Philadelphia, one for Cincinnati, and one for Baltimore. From 1938 until January 7, 1954, Atlantic City was the only city in the entire state of New Jersey to have modern trolley cars until January 8, 1954 when Public Service Coordinated Transport began operating President Conference Committee trolley cars in the Newark City Subway.

In 1945, the Atlantic City Transportation Company purchased the Atlantic Avenue line for $1 million and the interurban line in 1946 for $162,000. Trolley car service on the Atlantic Avenue line from the Inlet to Longport was every twelve minutes from 5 a.m. to 1:30 a.m. Extra cars were operated from the Inlet to the various cutback loops during peak periods. Around 1952, the Brilliners became known as the "Miss America Fleet." The Atlantic Avenue Line was cutback from Longport to the Douglas Avenue Loop on December 6, 1954.

The last day of the Atlantic Avenue trolley line was December 28, 1955. Car No. 207 was the last scheduled trolley car leaving the Inlet Terminus at 1:50 p.m. Immediately thereafter, a fleet of buses took over the service. However, at 3:30 p.m. on December 28, 1955, a trolley car parade of twelve Brilliners and eight "Hog Island" cars left the Douglas Avenue Loop and operated on Atlantic Avenue. Fourteen of the cars were chartered by civic and business groups at a cost of $100 per car. Six cars were available for the general public at a $2 per person fare, with proceeds benefitting the Atlantic City Hospital Building Fund. Uniformed nurses collected the fares, and other young women served as hostesses in each car. High school bands provided music with emphasis on "The Trolley Song." In the evening, four additional cars were chartered by various groups with the last car returning to the car barn after midnight. With the end of Atlantic City trolley cars, Newark was the only remaining trolley car system in the state of New Jersey until the Hudson–Bergen Light Rail Line (HBLR) opened on April 15, 2000. New Jersey Transit acquired the Atlantic City franchise in March 1985.

Virginia Avenue in Atlantic City is the location of this vintage trolley car around 1907. This was part of the Central Passenger Railway, a subsidiary of the West Jersey & Seashore Railroad that operated on Virginia Avenue to the Boardwalk.

Two trolley cars are at the wharf in Longport, which was a transfer point for Ocean City, New Jersey, boats in this 1910 postcard scene. (*Craig Knox collection*)

Longport, a borough in Atlantic County along the Atlantic Ocean Shore of Absecon Island, is the location on July 21, 1940 of Brilliner No. 6902 (later renumbered 202). (*Charlie Houser Sr. photograph, Craig Knox collection*)

With "Special" on the front destination sign around 1950, ACTC car No. 6890 might be on a chartered excursion. This double-truck, double-end, thirteen-window car was built by J. G. Brill Company in 1923. (*Craig Knox collection*)

The large Captain Starn's restaurant sign in the background in the Inlet section of Atlantic City is the location of ACTC car No. 6890. Clarence Starn opened the seafood restaurant on June 26, 1940. Over the years, it evolved to include speed boats, deep-sea fishing charters, live dolphins, a seafood market, and packing house to process the fish caught from his fleet. (*Craig Knox collection*)

Around 1952, ACTC cars (from right to left) Brilliner No. 207 (originally No. 6907) with the front destination sign showing "Inlet", Hog Island type car No. 250 (originally No. 6890) with the front destination sign showing "Douglas Avenue," and another Brilliner behind it are at the Inlet Loop in Atlantic City. Behind the cars is the Captain Starn's Restaurant. (*Craig Knox collection*)

In the early 1950s, ACTC car No. 250 (originally built by J. G. Brill Company in 1918 and became No. 6850 and later No. 250) followed by a Brilliner are at the Inlet in Atlantic City with the Captain Starn's sign in the background. After Clarence Starn died in 1969, the business went into decline, and the site was bulldozed in 1992. (*Craig Knox collection*)

ACTC car No. 6890 is on Atlantic Avenue around 1950. (*Craig Knox collection*)

On the center private right of way of Atlantic Avenue around 1950, car No. 6890 shows Douglas Avenue on the front destination sign. This was a cutback loop in the city of Margate. (*Craig Knox collection*)

An ACTC motorman poses at the doorway of car No. 6887 on June 8, 1952. This car was built by J. G. Brill Company in 1918 to serve the Hog Island Shipyard in Southwest Philadelphia. (*Charlie Houser Sr. photograph, Craig Knox collection*)

This was the first Brilliner car No. 6891 (renumbered 6901 and later renumbered 201) delivered to Atlantic City in 1938 by the J. G. Brill Company. Longport and Ventnor are printed above the windows. (*Clifford R. Scholes photograph, Craig Knox collection*)

In 1949, ACTC car No. 6885 is on Atlantic Avenue. This car was built by J. G. Brill Company in 1918 to transport workers to Philadelphia's Hog Island Shipyard and was acquired in 1923. (*Clifford R. Scholes photograph, Craig Knox collection*)

ACTC car No. 286 is about to pass a Brilliner on Atlantic Avenue in Atlantic City in 1952. (*Clifford R. Scholes photograph, Craig Knox collection*)

In 1952, ACTC Brilliner No. 204 (originally No. 6904) is near the Inlet Loop in Atlantic City. (*Clifford R. Scholes photograph, Craig Knox collection*)

Traveling on private right of way, car No. 286 provided dependable service on the Atlantic City to Longport line in 1952. (*Clifford R. Scholes photograph, Craig Knox collection*)

In 1952, the private right of way in the center of Atlantic Avenue near the Douglas Loop provided a traffic free transit ride for ACTC car No. 6839 built by the J. G. Brill Company in 1913. (*Clifford R. Scholes photograph, Craig Knox collection*)

Waiting for departure time, ACTC Brilliner car No. 207 (originally No. 6907) is at the Douglas Avenue Loop ready to turn on to Atlantic Avenue for its next trip through Atlantic City to Inlet Loop in 1952. (*Clifford R. Scholes photograph, Craig Knox collection*)

In the Inlet neighborhood of Atlantic City, ACTC Brilliner car No. 209 (originally No. 6909) in 1952 is near the Inlet terminus. (*Clifford R. Scholes photograph, Craig Knox collection*)

ACTC Brilliner car No. 225 (originally No. 6925) is on Vermont Avenue near the Inlet Loop in 1952. (*Clifford R. Scholes photograph, Craig Knox collection*)

Advertising the Steel Pier and a variety of items, ACTC car No. 6847 (originally car No. 146 built in 1918 by J. G. Brill Company for the Ocean Electric Railway of Rockaway, New York) is near the Inlet Car Barn in 1952. Built on iron pilings with a concrete understructure, the 1,000-foot-long Steel Pier opened on June 18, 1898. The trolley car line contributed to Atlantic City business by bringing in customers to the Atlantic City Business and Boardwalk area. (*Clifford R. Scholes photograph, Craig Knox collection*)

ACTC Brilliner No. 204 (originally No. 6904) is waiting for departure time, and the front destination sign reads "Ventnor-Margate, Douglas Avenue Only" around 1952. (*George Conrad collection, Craig Knox collection*)

In the early 1950s, ACTC Brilliner No. 219 (originally No. 6919) is at Longport waiting for departure time for the next trip to the Inlet in Atlantic City. The station shelter was similar to many of the shelters on the Shore Fast Line. (*David H. Cope photograph, Richard L. Allman collection, Craig Knox collection*)

On July 5, 1952, ACTC Brilliner No. 213 (originally No. 6913) is on the double-track section at Longport along the Great Egg Harbor Inlet. (*R.L. Long photograph, Craig Knox collection*)

Around 1952, ACTC Brilliner No. 223 (originally No. 6923) is on Atlantic Avenue heading for Longport. (*Craig Knox collection*)

ACTC car No. 6890 is on Atlantic Avenue in Atlantic City around 1952. (*Craig Knox collection*)

Car No. 6888 is in the loop with Margate on the front destination sign around 1952. (*Craig Knox collection*)

In the early 1950s, an ACTC Brilliner is on the reserved right of way along Atlantic Avenue on the bayside of the Atlantic Ocean. (*Joseph F. Eid Jr. curator, Craig Knox collection*)

An ACTC Brilliner is providing a scenic view of the bay for passengers on its trip to Atlantic City gliding over the private right of way parallel to Atlantic Avenue around 1952. (*Joseph F. Eid Jr. curator, Craig Knox collection*)

In 1952, ACTC No. 219 is at the Inlet station awaiting the next trip to Atlantic City. (*Charlie Houser Sr. photograph, Craig Knox collection*)

An ACTC Brilliner is at a passenger stop on Atlantic Avenue with the front destination sign showing Margate-Longport in 1952. (*Craig Knox collection*)

In 1952, ACTC Brilliner No. 225 (originally No. 6925) is on private right of way in Atlantic City. (*Clifford R. Scholes photograph, Craig Knox collection*)

ACTC Brilliner No. 217 (originally No. 6917) is on the traffic free private right of way in the center of Atlantic Avenue in 1952. (*Clifford R. Scholes photograph, Craig Knox collection*)

Track in the street and overhear wire provide positive identity of the public transit line for ACTC Brilliner No. 223 on Atlantic Avenue in Atlantic City in 1952. (*Clifford R. Scholes photograph, Craig Knox collection*)

In 1952, Longport station shelter is the location of ACTC Brilliner No. 212 (originally No. 6912). (*Clifford R. Scholes photograph, Craig Knox collection*)

In March 1954, ACTC Brilliner No. 225 is boarding passengers at Longport for the trip to Atlantic City. (*Bob's Photos collection*)

ACTC Brilliner No. 207 is travelling on the private right of way along the Atlantic Ocean shoreline from Longport to Atlantic City on August 22, 1954. (*Bob's Photos collection*)

ACTC car No. 6888 is on private right of way in Atlantic City around 1955. (*Clifford R. Scholes photograph, Craig Knox collection*)

On September 25, 1955, ACTC car No. 6890 is traversing the center of the road private right of way section of the Atlantic City–Longport Line. (*Clifford R. Scholes photograph, Craig Knox collection*)

ACTC car No. 250 (originally No. 6850) is at the Inlet Car Barn in 1955. (*Clifford R. Scholes photograph, Craig Knox collection*)

In 1955, Douglas Avenue Loop is the location of ACTC Brilliner No. 203 (originally No. 6903) with Inlet on the front destination sign and behind it is car No. 6888. (*Clifford R. Scholes photograph, Craig Knox collection*)

ACTC Brilliner No. 224 (originally No. 6924) followed by a Hog Island type of car and behind it another Brilliner are at the Inlet Car Barn waiting for the next assignment in 1955. (*Clifford R. Scholes photograph, Craig Knox collection*)

In 1955, ACTC Hog Island type car No. 6888 is on the private right of way section of the line in Atlantic City. (*Clifford R. Scholes photograph, Craig Knox collection*)

ACTC car No. 6888 is in its last year of operation on Atlantic Avenue in Atlantic City in 1955. (*Clifford R. Scholes photograph, Craig Knox collection*)

On September 25, 1955, ACTC car No. 6890 is passing through a neat residential area on Atlantic Avenue with nothing showing for a destination. (*Craig Knox collection*)

ACTC car No. 6890 is at a passenger stop on Atlantic Avenue on September 25, 1955. (*Craig Knox collection*)

On December 18, 1955, car No. 6888 is at the Douglas Avenue Loop. (*Bill Milow photograph*)

Hog Island type car No. 250 is at the Inlet Car Barn in Atlantic City ready for the next assignment on December 18, 1955. (*Bill Milow photograph*)

ACTC Brilliner No. 213 has just past a J. G. Brill Company-built car that has just made a stop on Atlantic Avenue on December 23, 1955. Only five days were left before the last day of trolley car operation in Atlantic City on December 28, 1955. (*Bob's Photos collection*)

On December 28, 1955, the last day of trolley car operation in Atlantic City, Brilliner No. 201, with "The Miss America Fleet" painted above the side windows just behind the front entranceway door, is on Atlantic Avenue in Atlantic City with the destination sign showing "Douglas Avenue." (*Bill Milow photograph*)

This picture of the front of Brilliner No. 219 on Atlantic Avenue was taken out of the back window of another trolley car on December 28, 1955, the last day of Atlantic City trolley car operation. (*Bob's Photos collection*)

A 6800 series car built by J. G. Brill Company may be posing for a picture on this last day of trolley car operation in Atlantic City on December 28, 1955. (*Bob's Photos collection*)

Brilliner No. 207 is at Longport for the public to get their last look at the trolley car on December 28, 1955. (*Charlie Houser Sr. photograph, Craig Knox collection*)

ACTC car No. 6887 (built by J. G. Brill Company in 1918) is at an Atlantic Avenue passenger stop on the last day of trolley car service December 28, 1955. The car had been autographed with numerous comments, including "Sentimental Journey" on the front and side of the car. (*Charlie Houser Sr. photograph, Craig Knox collection*)

"Good Bye trolley cars" attached to the side of Brilliner No. 219 was an excellent way to sum up December 28, 1955, the last day of Atlantic City trolley car service. New Jersey Transit bus route 505 basically covers the former trolley route. The January 14, 2017 schedule showed the full length of the line is from Atlantic Avenue at 16th Avenue in Longport via Ventnor Avenue and Atlantic Avenue through downtown Atlantic City to W. Riverside Drive at Murray Avenue in the Venice Park neighborhood of Atlantic City. Additional service operated from Ventnor Avenue at Franklin Avenue in Margate to Atlantic Avenue at S. Carolina Avenue in downtown Atlantic City. (*Craig Knox collection*)

3

Five Mile Beach Electric Railway

The Five Mile Beach Electric Railway opened June 10, 1903 with free rides and began revenue service on June 11, 1903. The route started at Pine Avenue on New Jersey Avenue in Anglesea heading southeast on New Jersey Avenue, turning left on to 1st Avenue, right on to Atlantic Avenue, south on Atlantic Avenue, turning right at Schellenger Avenue, left on Pacific Avenue, curved right on to Rio Grande Avenue, and ended at the edge of the Grassy Sound Channel. In 1906, track was extended southward on Pacific Avenue from Rio Grande Avenue to the Wildwood Crest boundary, turned right on to Rambler Road, and ended at the ferry wharf for the Sewell's Point Ferry. The hour-long round trip required eight cars for a seven-minute, thirty-second headway in the summer. Winter service required two cars for a thirty-minute headway. The Atlantic City Electric Company acquired the line in 1924 and sold it in 1928 to the American Gas and Electric Company. It was purchased by the Central Public Service Corporation in 1929. The Manhattan Bus Company purchased the line in 1943, and the line was converted to bus operation in 1945.

In July 1936, single-truck, double-ended, nine-bench open car No. 36, built by J. G. Brill Company, is at Wildwood Crest waiting for departure time. (*Craig Knox collection*)

On July 1, 1939, nine-bench open car No. 32 is at North Wildwood, New Jersey. This was one of three cars (Nos. 30, 32, and 34) built by Jackson and Sharp Company. (*S.D. Maguire photograph, Craig Knox collection*)

Open car No. 20 and another open car passing at North Wildwood on August 4, 1940. (*S.D. Maguire photograph, Craig Knox collection*)

Pacific Avenue at Morninglory Road in Wildwood, New Jersey, is the location of an open car on September 1, 1941. (*Craig Knox collection*)

Double-truck, double-ended, twelve-bench open car No. 27 built by J. G. Brill Company is at North Wildwood, New Jersey, on August 4, 1940. (*S.D. Maguire photograph, Craig Knox collection*)

In 1941 on Pacific Avenue, a twelve-bench open car is on the Five Mile Beach Electric Railway at Wildwood Crest, New Jersey. (*Don Wentzel photograph, Craig Knox collection*)

Three open cars are at a passenger stop on Atlantic Avenue at Glenwood in Wildwood, New Jersey, in 1941. (*Harold A. Smith photograph, Craig Knox collection*)

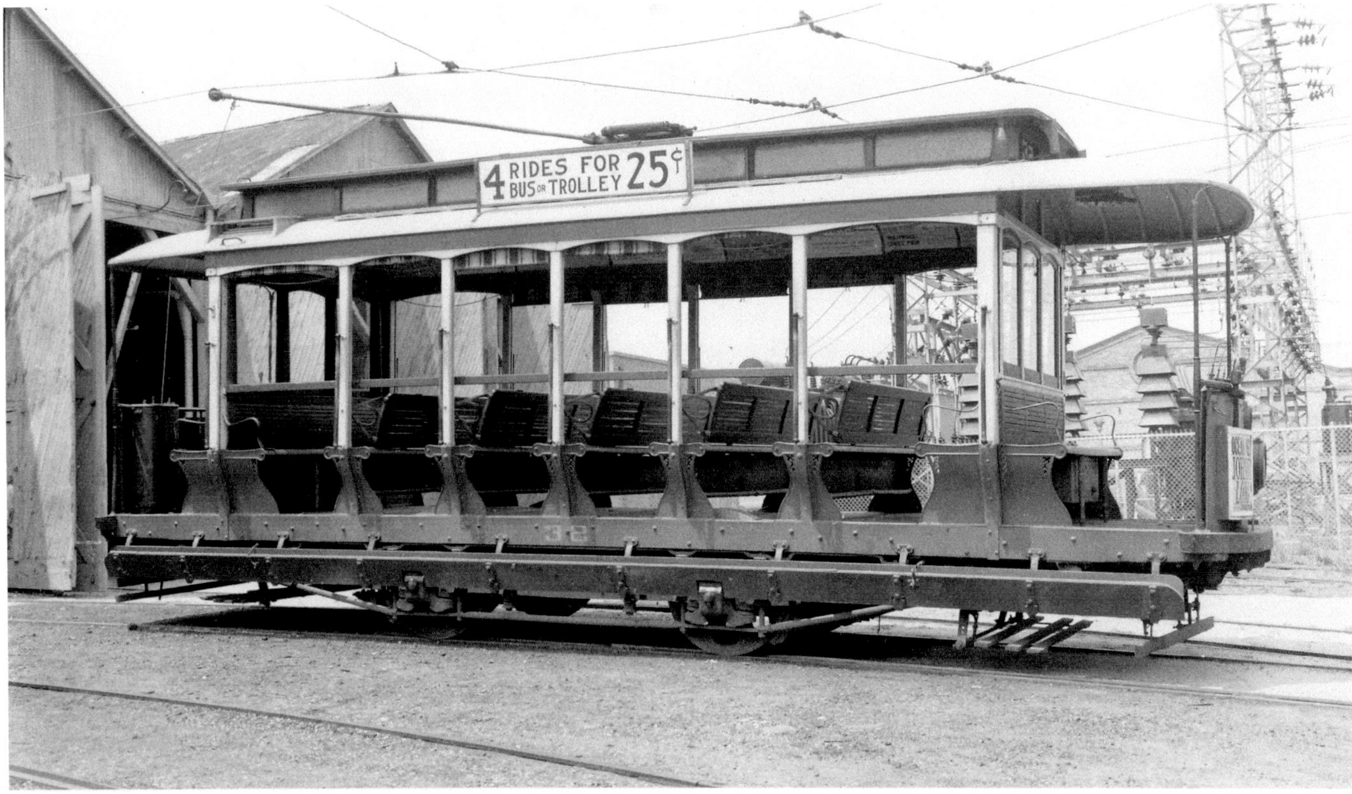

On July 20, 1940, car No. 32 is at the Wildwood car barn waiting for the next assignment. This was one of three single-truck open cars (Nos. 30, 32, and 34) suited for summer weather in Wildwood built between 1899 and 1901 at the Delaware Car Works in Wilmington, Delaware, by the Jackson & Sharp Company. (*Craig Knox collection*)

Double-truck, double-end, twelve-bench open car No. 22 is on Pacific Avenue at Morninglory Road in Wildwood on September 1, 1941. (*Craig Knox collection*)

Three single-truck open cars are at Wildwood Crest on August 17, 1941. (*S.D. Maguire photograph, Craig Knox collection*)

North Wildwood is the location of this double-truck car in North Wildwood on September 5, 1943. (*S.D. Maguire photograph, Craig Knox collection*)

4

Pennsylvania–Reading Seashore Lines

Atlantic City and the South Jersey seashore became major vacation destinations for Philadelphia-area residents with two competing railroads linking Camden with southern New Jersey resorts. On May 4, 1896, the Pennsylvania Railroad consolidated all of its railroads in southern New Jersey into the West Jersey & Seashore Railroad. The line from Camden via Newfield and Millville to Atlantic City was electrified at 650 volts DC and opened on September 10, 1906 with cars that looked like wooden interurban trolley cars. Eight days later, steam passenger trains on that line were retired. However, freight trains continued to be moved by steam locomotives. A third rail system was installed for the line except overhead wire was installed from Mickle Street in Camden to Gloucester City and along the 10-mile section between Newfield and Millville. The West Jersey & Seashore Railroad competed with the Atlantic City Railroad owned by the Philadelphia & Reading Company. In many areas, the two lines were very close together, and trains sometimes raced one another to see which would be the first to arrive at their destination. The opening of the Delaware River Bridge (a suspension bridge across the Delaware River connecting Philadelphia, Pennsylvania, with Camden, New Jersey) on July 1, 1926 made it easier for southeastern Pennsylvania residents to drive to Atlantic City and other New Jersey seashore points. In addition, the White Horse Pike became a first-class highway from Camden to Atlantic City. Direct bus service between areas in Camden, Salem, Cumberland, and Gloucester counties to Philadelphia attracted former railroad passengers. Over a period of time, railroad commuter service and passenger service between Philadelphia and Atlantic City declined. Electrified service between Newfield and Atlantic City was terminated on September 18, 1931.

On March 4, 1931, the New Jersey Board of Public Utilities ordered the two railroad companies to join their southern New Jersey lines into one company. State approval occurred on April 11, 1933 followed by Interstate Commerce Commission approval on June 10, 1933. Combined operations began on June 25, 1933 under the Pennsylvania–Reading Seashore Lines (PRSL). The Pennsylvania Railroad had two-thirds ownership and the Reading Railroad had one-third ownership.

New Jersey's public utility regulators ordered PRSL on October 20, 1948 to remove its twenty-six remaining wooden multiple-unit coaches from service because of collision and fire concerns. In the fall of 1948, electrified commuter service was cut back to operate from Camden to Glassboro, and that service ended on September 8, 1949. In September 1949, the Budd Company introduced the self-propelled rail diesel car (RDC). PRSL acquired twelve RDC-1 cars (all passenger coach seating ninety passengers). Numbered M402–M413, the first six arrived on October 18, 1950, and the remaining six arrived in May 1951.

The Nellie Bly, the last New York City–Atlantic City passenger train made its final run on April 29, 1961. Non-electrified commuter service from Camden to Glassboro ended on March 5, 1971. On February 27, 1965, the Pennsylvania–Reading Seashore Lines (PRSL) closed their terminal at Arkansas and Atlantic Avenues in Atlantic City that had opened in 1934 with their last outbound train leaving at 7:20 a.m. That same day, the first inbound train arrived at 10:05 a.m. at a new smaller three-track terminal located one block away at Arctic and Arkansas Avenues. The old station (built with eight passenger tracks) had been purchased by the Atlantic City Development Authority for conversion into a bus terminal. It had originally replaced the steam railroad West Jersey & Seashore (WJ&S) station at South Carolina and Atlantic Avenues along with the Tennessee and Atlantic Avenues station of the WJ&S Newfield electric line. The completion of the Atlantic City Expressway in July 1965 continued the decline of passenger service. Final PRSL service into Camden, which operated between West Haddonfield and Camden, ended on January 14, 1966. The Somers Point branch was cut back to Linwood on August 4, 1944. Passenger service on the Pemberton Branch between Camden and Pemberton ended on April 25, 1969. New Jersey Transit took over passenger operations of PRSL and Conrail on September 16, 1978. Passenger service to Atlantic City ended because of poor track conditions on June 30, 1982.

On May 23, 1989, Amtrak reopened the Atlantic City Line for service to Atlantic City; however, on April 2, 1995, New Jersey Transit became the sole provider of railroad passenger service to Atlantic City. The July 28, 2019 New Jersey Transit rail schedule between Philadelphia and Atlantic City shows twelve daily trains in each direction.

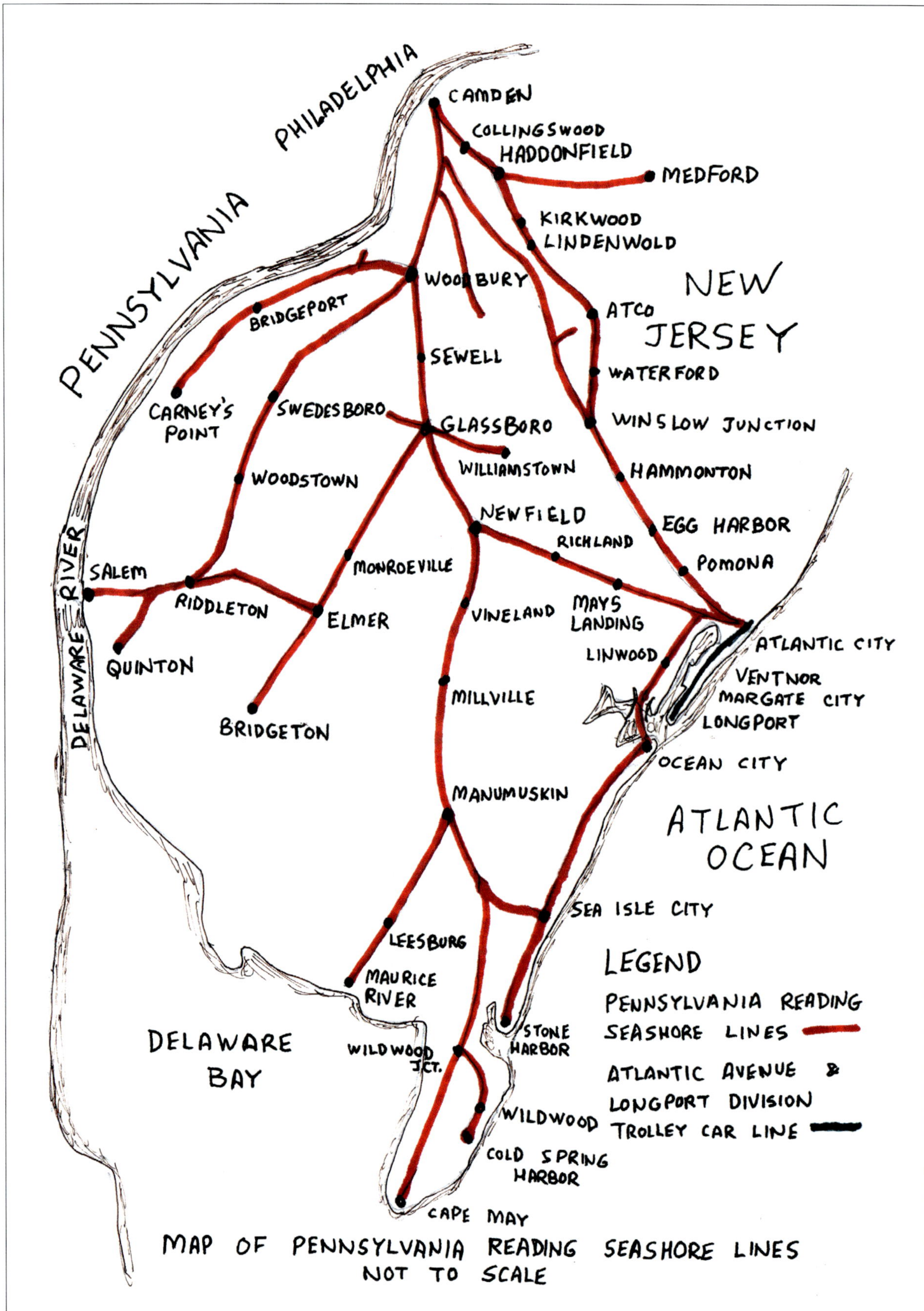

This is a map of the Pennsylvania-Reading Seashore Lines created in 1933 as a consolidation of Pennsylvania Railroad and Reading Company lines in southern New Jersey.

The Pennsylvania-Reading Seashore Lines completed their new brick faced Atlantic City Station located at Arkansas and Atlantic Avenues on February 12, 1935 shown in this postcard view. This replaced three Atlantic City passenger stations. The Reading Railroad used a station at Atlantic and Arkansas Avenues. Pennsylvania Railroad steam trains had a station at South Carolina and Atlantic Avenues. Electrified train service, before it ended on September 18, 1931, used a station at Tennessee and Atlantic Avenues.

PRSL locomotive No. 5710 with a 4-6-0 wheel arrangement known as a ten wheeler is at the 4th Street Station in Ocean City in August 1950. This was one of ninety G5s-class locomotives built between 1923 and 1925 at the Pennsylvania Railroad Juniata Shops. One of these locomotives, No. 5741, has been preserved at the Railroad Museum of Pennsylvania. (*H. Gerald Mac Donald Graphic Arts, Craig Knox collection*)

In August 1950, PRSL class E6s locomotive No. 1238 is at 10th Street in Ocean City. This Atlantic type locomotive with a 4-4-2 wheel arrangement was built at the Pennsylvania Railroad Juniata Shop in May 1914. Atlantic-type locomotives were noted for speed and handled many of the New Jersey seashore routes. This locomotive was retired in April 1951. (*H. Gerald Mac Donald Graphic Arts, Craig Knox collection*)

At the 4th Street yard in Ocean City (from left to right), PRSL locomotives Nos. 1238 and 5710 are waiting for their next assignment in August 1950. (*H. Gerald Mac Donald Graphic Arts, Craig Knox collection*)

CAPE MAY, WILDWOOD, STONE HARBOR, SEA ISLE CITY and OCEAN CITY to CAMDEN, PHILADELPHIA

Eastern Standard Time	304 Except Sat., Sun. & Nov.24, Dec. 26 and Jan. 2 A	406 Sat. only A	416 Except Sun. & Nov.24, Dec. 26 and Jan. 2 A	424 Sun. & Nov.24, Dec. 26 and Jan. 2 A
	AM NB	AM NB	PM NB	PM NB
Lv **Cape May**	6.22	6.41	3.03	6.18
" Erma (Bennett)	f 6.29	f 6.48	f 3.10	f 6.25
" Wildwood—Rio Grande	6.32	6.51	3.13	6.28
Ar Wildwood Junction	6.35	6.54	3.16	6.31
Lv Wildwood Junction	6.36			
" West Wildwood				
Ar Wildwood (Oak Avenue)	6.44			
Lv **Wildwood** (Oak Avenue)	6.46			
" West Wildwood	a 6.48			
Ar Wildwood Junction	6.54			
Lv **Wildwood Junction**	6.54	6.54	3.16	6.31
" Whitesboro			f 3.18	
" **Cape May Court House**	7.00	7.00	3.23	6.37
" Woodbine Jct. (Woodbine)	f 7.14	f 7.14	f 3.37	f 6.51
Ar Tuckahoe				
Bus on Public Highway: Lv Stone Harbor (96th St. between 2nd & 3rd Ave.)	6.12	6.12		
" Avalon (21st St. & 2nd Ave.)	6.25	6.25		
" Avalon (6th St. & 2nd Ave.)	6.30	6.30		
" Townsend Inlet (86th St. & Landis Ave.)	6.35	6.35		
" **Sea Isle City** (41st St. & Landis Ave.)	6.43	6.43		
" Strathmere (Tecumsha Ave.)	6.50	6.50		
Ar **Ocean City** (51st Street)	6.59	6.59		
Ocean City				
Lv **10th Street**	6.52	6.52	3.12	6.28
" 14th Street	f 6.55	f 6.55	3.14	6.30
" 24th Street	f 6.58	f 6.58	f 3.17	f 6.33
" 34th Street	f 7.00	f 7.00	f 3.20	f 6.36
" **51st Street**	7.04	7.04	3.24	6.40
" Palermo	f 7.09	f 7.09	f 3.29	f 6.45
" Petersburg	f 7.13	f 7.13	f 3.33	f 6.49
Ar **Tuckahoe**	7.18	7.18	3.40	6.56
Lv **Tuckahoe**	7.18	7.18	3.40	6.56
Ar Haddonfield	8.07	8.07	4.30	7.45
Ar **Camden** (Broadway) (■)	8.15	8.15	4.39	7.54
Philadelphia				
Ar Frankford Junction	dq8.30	dq8.30	dq4.54	dq8.07
" North Philadelphia	q 8.36	q 8.36	q 5.00	q 8.15
Ar Pennsylvania Station (30th St.)	q 8.46	q 8.46	q 5.10	q 8.25
	AM	AM	PM	PM

REFERENCE NOTES

■—Subway-High Speed Line from or to subway stations in Philadelphia offers convenient connections at Broadway, Camden, with trains to and from New Jersey points.

A—Passengers for Frankford Junction, North Philadelphia and Pennsylvania Station (30th Street) Philadelphia change trains at Haddonfield.

E—Will not run on Nov. 24, Dec. 26, Jan. 2 and Feb. 22.

H—Will not run on Nov. 24, Dec. 26 and Jan. 2.

NB—No checked baggage handled on this train.

a—Stops only on signal or notice to Agent to receive passengers.

d—Stops only to discharge passengers.

f—Stops only on signal or notice to Agent or Conductor to receive or discharge passengers.

k—Stops Saturdays only.

q—Passengers change at Haddonfield.

PHILADELPHIA, CAMDEN to OCEAN CITY, SEA ISLE CITY, STONE HARBOR, WILDWOOD and CAPE MAY

Miles	Eastern Standard Time	409 Except Sun. & Nov.24, Dec. 26 and Jan. 2	427 Sat. only	331 Except Sat., Sun. & Nov.24, Dec. 26 and Jan. 2	433 Sun. & Nov.24, Dec. 26 and Jan. 2
		AM NB	PM NB	PM NB	PM NB
	Philadelphia				
	Lv Penna. Station (30th St.)	q 8.20	q 4.45	q 4.45	q 8.05
	" North Philadelphia	q 8.30	q 4.55	q 4.55	q 8.15
	" Frankford Junction	cq 8.36	cq 5.01	cq 5.01	
.0	Lv **Camden** (Broadway) (■)	8.53	5.24	5.24	8.39
6.5	" Haddonfield	9.01	5.32	5.32	8.47
54.3	Ar **Tuckahoe**	9.47	6.18	6.18	9.33
54.3	Lv **Tuckahoe**	9.50	6.21	6.21	9.36
57.6	" Petersburg	f 9.56	f 6.27	f 6.27	f 9.42
60.6	" Palermo	f10.01	f 6.31	f 6.31	f 9.46
	Ocean City				
63.0	" **51st Street**	10.05	6.36	6.36	9.51
64.8	" 34th Street	f10.09	f 6.40	f 6.40	f 9.55
65.9	" 24th Street	10.12	6.43	6.43	9.58
66.9	" 14th Street	10.15	f 6.46	f 6.46	10.01
67.4	Ar **10th Street**	10.18	6.49	6.49	10.04
	Bus on Public Highway: Lv **Ocean City** (51st Street)		6.37	6.37	
	Ar Strathmere (Tecumsha Ave.)		6.46	6.46	
	" **Sea Isle City** (41st St. & Landis Ave.)		6.53	6.53	
	" Townsend Inlet (86th St. & Landis Ave.)		7.01	7.01	
	" Avalon (6th St. & 2nd Ave.)		7.06	7.06	
	" Avalon (21st St. & 2nd Ave.)		7.11	7.11	
	Ar Stone Harbor (96th St. between 2nd & 3rd Ave.)		7.24	7.24	
54.3	Lv Tuckahoe	9.47	6.18	6.18	9.33
58.6	" Woodbine Jct. (Woodbine)	9.53	6.24	6.24	f 9.39
69.4	" **Cape May Court House**	10.07	6.38	6.38	9.52
72.6	" Whitesboro	f10.11			
73.5	Ar **Wildwood Junction**	10.14	6.45	6.45	9.58
73.5	Lv Wildwood Junction			6.45	
76.3	" West Wildwood			b 6.51	
77.5	Ar **Wildwood** (Oak Avenue)			6.57	
	Lv Wildwood (Oak Avenue)			6.58	
	" West Wildwood				
	Ar Wildwood Junction			7.06	
73.5	Lv Wildwood Junction	10.14	6.45	7.07	9.58
74.8	" Wildwood—Rio Grande	10.17	6.48	7.10	10.01
77.2	" Erma (Bennett)	f10.20	f 6.51	f 7.13	f10.04
81.2	Ar **Cape May**	10.27	6.58	7.20	10.11
		AM	PM	PM	PM

REFERENCE NOTES

■—Subway-High Speed Line from or to subway stations in Philadelphia offers convenient connections at Broadway, Camden, with trains to and from New Jersey points.

♥—These tickets are subject to 10% Federal Tax.

H—Will not run on Nov. 24, Dec. 26 and Jan. 2.

NB—No checked baggage handled on this train.

NK—No checked baggage handled on this train on Saturdays.

b—Stops only on notice to Conductor to discharge passengers.

c—Stops only to receive passengers.

f—Stops only on signal or notice to Agent or Conductor to receive or discharge passengers.

q—Passengers change at Haddonfield.

Printed in U.S.A. 1st edition 30M 10-6-60

This is a portion of the October 30, 1960 PRSL timetable for New Jersey train service from Philadelphia and Camden to Ocean City, Sea Isle City, Stone Harbor, Wildwood, and Cape May. At that time there also was service between 30th Street Station Philadelphia and Atlantic City via North Philadelphia, Frankford Junction, Haddonfield, Hammonton, and Egg Harbor. A few trips existed between Camden and Atlantic City. There was between Camden and Millville three Monday-Friday trips in each direction and one trip in each direction on Saturday. Between Camden and Hammonton, there was one Monday-Friday trip in each direction.

A PRSL rail diesel car (RDC) is at Wildwood waiting for departure time. Between 1950 and 1951, PRSL acquired twelve rail diesel cars (Nos. M-402–M-413, model RDC-1), each seating eighty-nine passengers from the Budd Company of Philadelphia. (*Craig Knox collection*)

On August 16, 1997, a Cape May Seashore Lines (CMSL) RDC is at the County Park in New Jersey. CMSL began train service between Cape May Court House and Cold Spring Valley, New Jersey, in 1996. (*Kenneth C. Springirth photograph*)

5

Route 7 City Subway in Newark

In November 1831, the 90 mile-Morris Canal, owned by the Morris Canal & Banking Company, opened between Phillipsburg and Newark, New Jersey. In 1836, the canal was extended eastward from Newark to Jersey City. By 1860, the canal was enlarged for larger boats and barges. After the Civil War, railroads became the major freight hauler and the Morris Canal lost most of its freight business. On November 24, 1903, Public Service Corporation President Thomas N. McCarter recommended a streetcar subway in Newark to alleviate surface traffic. With nothing happening, McCarter sent a message to Newark Mayor Haussling on December 22, 1910, noting that in the last five years, the number of streetcars passing Broad and Market Streets increased from 387 cars per hour to 525 and recommended, "If possible, the Morris Canal should be abandoned and its roadbed, from the Pennsylvania Railroad westward, should be utilized as an open air subway." Public Service Corporation organized the Public Service Railway Company on August 20, 1907. In 1922, the ownership of the Morris Canal & Banking Company passed to the state of New Jersey. On March 12, 1924, New Jersey legislators voted to end the Morris Canal. In the spring of 1924, water was drained from the canal bed, and the Newark portion was set aside to be used for a streetcar line.

On February 11, 1927, Public Service Railway Company announced that the words "Public Service" painted on the sides of the cars would be replaced by a public service emblem in the center of the vehicle sides. The emblem was a circular blue band with the words "Public Service" in gold letters and enclosed a red triangle on a white field. At the same time, route numbers were established for bus and trolley lines. On January 31, 1928, Public Service Coordinated Transport took over the Public Service Railway Company. A ground breaking was conducted on Central Avenue and Norfolk Street in Newark on November 18, 1929. Once dredging and plowing operations were completed, concrete overpasses, station platforms, and stairways were built for important streets. Track gauge was standard railroad gauge 4 feet 8.5 inches. From Warren Street to Orange Street, the line was in an open cut with concrete retaining walls making some turns following the original canal bed. Orange Street was the only grade crossing on the line. After crossing Orange Street, the line bridged the electrified Delaware Lackawanna & Western Railroad. The reason for the Orange Street grade crossing was to avoid a grade crossing with the railroad. From Orange Street to Heller Parkway, the line followed a northward course. Costing $5 million, the line featured well-ballasted track and had an automatic signal system. Stations were Newark Penn Station, Broad Street, Washington Street, Warren Street, Norfolk Street, Orange Street, Park Avenue, Bloomfield Avenue, Davenport Avenue, Heller Parkway, and Franklin Avenue.

On October 3, 1934, a trial run was made using a Public Service 6500-type gasoline car. Overhead wire installation began in November 1934. On May 26, 1935, Public Service Coordinated Traction Route 29 (Bloomfield Avenue) trolley car No. 2713 made the first trip operating between Broad Street and Heller Parkway. Service was extended into the new Pennsylvania Railroad Station on June 20, 1937. A quarter-mile extension from Heller Parkway to Franklin Avenue opened on November 22, 1940, making the Route 7 City Subway line 4.25 miles long. The other lines using the subway were two branches of Route 21 (Orange), exiting at Warren and Orange Streets, and 23 (Central), exiting at the Norfolk Street ramp. Tracks were extended eastward underground to Pennsylvania Station. For a short time using the City Subway were Route 43 (Jersey City) that last operated as a trolley line on April 30, 1938, Route 13 (Broad) that last operated as a trolley line on September 4, 1937, and Route 27 (Mt. Prospect) that last operated as a trolley line on December 18, 1937. Route 43 was converted to trackless trolley operation, while Routes 13 and 27 were converted to bus operation.

On January 4, 1944, a serious accident occurred in the City Subway when Route 23 (Central) car No. 3215 jumped the track on a curve as it was coming into the Pennsylvania Railroad Station. The car jumped the tracks and tore along the tunnel wall for about 100 feet, injuring sixteen passengers. Cables were torn by the car and part of the tunnel was plunged into darkness. Flashlights were used to rescue the injured. With both ends of the car smashed in, the car was scrapped.

Route 23 was converted to bus operation on December 14, 1947. Public Service announced in August 1950 that Route 7 (City Subway) would remain a trolley car line; however, the remaining Newark trolley car lines would be converted to bus operation. Route 21 was converted west of Roseville carhouse and the West Market branch of Route 21 was converted on March 1, 1951. The rest of Route 21 and the entire Route 29 Bloomfield were converted on March 30, 1952, with car No. 2715 making the last trip on Route 21 and car No. 2725 made the last run on Route 29.

Route 7 trolley cars used Orange Street from the City Subway trackage to Roseville Car House. However, the opening of new shops below Penn Station on June 5, 1952 meant that trips were no longer made to the Roseville Car House. Route 7 operated a ten-minute headway during rush hours and a fifteen-minute headway in off-peak periods. After the conversion of Routes 21, 23, and 29 to bus service, service was increased on Route 7 from 114 to 180 daily trips.

Route 7 received thirty used single end PCC cars purchased for a total cost of $350,000 from the Twin City Rapid Transit Company of Minneapolis–St. Paul, which was in process of converting to an all bus operation. The first PCC car came to Newark on August 12, 1953 and became Public Service Coordinated Transport No. 21 repainted with a grey and white body, blue stripes, and red wheels and wings. A new trolley car loop was placed in service for the PCC cars on December 21, 1953, and the first PCC car was placed in service on January 8, 1954. By February 4, 1954, all of the older cars were no longer in service. With buses replacing Atlantic City trolleys on December 28, 1955, Newark City Subway was New Jersey's last electric trolley line until the new Hudson–Bergen Light Rail Line opened on April 15, 2000. On August 23, 1971, Public Service Coordinated Transport became Transport of New Jersey with the State of New Jersey subsidizing operation. When the State of New Jersey took over operation of the City Subway on October 14, 1980, it became New Jersey Transit.

Newark's PCC cars were carefully maintained. Every 1,500 miles, there were inspections of track brakes, torque arms, journal bearings, and wheels. The car body was checked including deadman controls, door mechanisms, motors, and batteries.

On August 24, 2001, a formal retirement ceremony was held at Branch Brook Park Station (formerly Franklin Avenue) at noon for the last day of PCC car operation. After forty-seven years of service, the twenty-four remaining PCC cars on Newark's City Subway made their last run. On August 27, 2001, sixteen new air-conditioned, three-sectional articulated cars (Nos. 101–116) built by Kinkisharyo (almost identical to the cars built for the Hudson-Bergen light rail system) went into service. Each car can seat sixty-eight passengers, accommodate two wheel chairs, and 122 passengers can stand in the vehicle. With the former loop removed, the new cars reversed at the Branch Brook Park Station; however, they still loop at Penn Station in Newark.

The route at the outer end has been changed by replacing the Heller Parkway and Franklin Avenue station by the new Branch Brook station. With the removal of the Franklin Avenue Loop, the line has been extended a few streets to enter the tracks of the Orange Branch of the Erie Railroad/Conrail and continues west for a short distance ending at Grove Street where a new carhouse and repair shop was built to service the new cars. A large park and ride lot was built adjacent to the Grove Street Terminal. This new facility replaced the storage and shop area under Penn Station in downtown Newark.

On July 17, 2006, a 1.1-mile line opened connecting the Amtrak/NJ Transit Northeast Corridor Station (Former Pennsylvania Railroad Newark Station) with the NJ Transit North Newark railroad station (Morris & Essex Railroad/Delaware Lackawanna & Western Railroad) at Broad and Orange Streets. Just west of the former Pennsylvania Railroad Newark Station, the line turns into a new cut-and-cover tunnel and ramps up to the surface on the west side of the intersection of Center Street and New Jersey Highway Route 21 McCarter Highway. It continues on the west side of McCarter Highway. At Lombardy Street, the line splits with the northbound track on Atlantic Street, which has two stations, Atlantic Street and Riverfront Stadium. The southbound track uses Broad Street which has a station at Washington Park. Broad Street is crossed on a diagonal after Riverfront Station, and the line ends at a double-track terminus with a scissors crossover and converges into a single track at the Broad Street Station. The new line serves Newark City Library, Newark Historical Society, Newark Museum, and a professional minor league baseball stadium.

For fiscal year 2017 (July 1, 2016 to June 30, 2017), the Newark City Subway for an average weekday handled 19,573 passengers, average Saturday handled 6,622 passengers, and average Sunday handled 4,108 passengers. This line has twenty-one cars built by Kinkisharyo that are owned and operated by the Central Division of New Jersey Transit Bus operations.

In 2019, the Newark City Subway is a light rail line running underground downtown and at grade level in outlying areas. Between Grove Street and Newark Penn Station service effective April 7, 2018 was as follows: Monday to Friday approximately every ten minutes off peak, and seven to ten minutes morning and afternoon peak. Morning and afternoon peak period between Branch Brook Park and Newark Penn Station was every three to five minutes. Evening service between Grove Street and Newark Penn Station generally has a longer time interval, Saturday service was every twenty minutes, and Sunday service was every twenty-five minutes. On the Broad Street–Penn Station line, Monday to Friday midday service every thirty minutes; morning and afternoon peak service was every thirteen to seventeen minutes, with the last trip leaving Broad Street Station at 11:44 p.m.; Saturday service was every twenty minutes, with last trip leaving Broad Street Station 11:39 p.m.; and Sunday service every twenty-five minutes, with the last trip leaving Broad Street Station at 11:20 p.m.

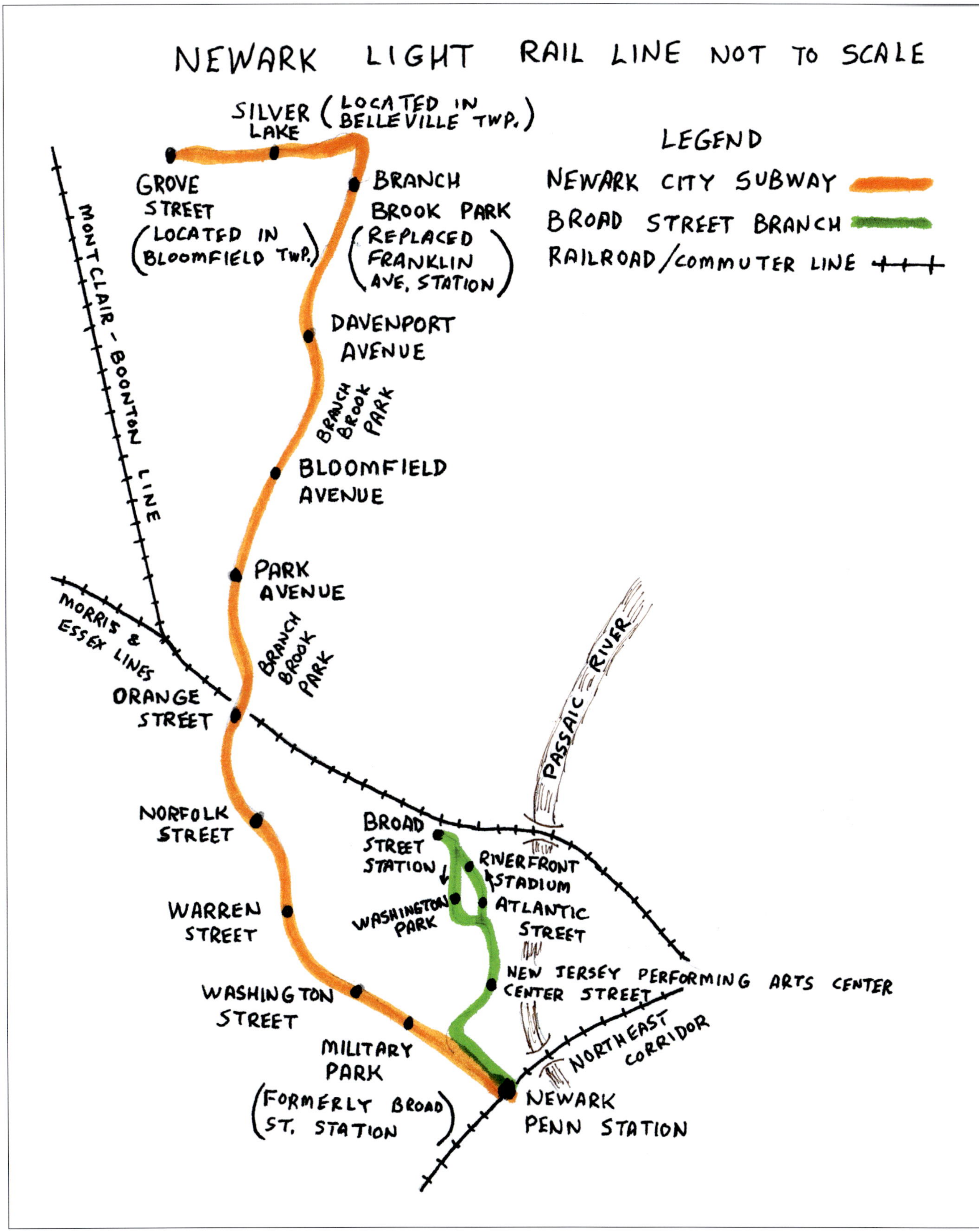

This map shows the Newark Light Rail system. On June 22, 2002, the Newark City Subway was extended from Branch Brook Park to Grove Street. The 1.1-mile Broad Street Extension opened July 17, 2006 connecting Newark Penn Station (originally owned by the Pennsylvania Railroad) to the Broad Street Station (originally owned by the Delaware, Lackawanna & Western Railroad and later Erie Lackawanna Railroad).

Newark City Subway car No. 8011 is at the Franklin Avenue Station on September 20, 1955. This double-truck car was originally car No. 2712, one of thirty-eight cars (Nos. 2701–2738) built by Cincinnati Car Company in 1918 for Public Service Railway Company. It was later renumbered 8011. Cincinnati Car Company of Cincinnati, Ohio, was founded in 1902 and ended operation in 1938. (*Clifford R. Scholes photograph*)

In February 1961, Newark City Subway PCC cars No. 10 (originally Twin City Rapid Transit Company [TCRTC] of Minneapolis, Minnesota, No. 329) and No. 13 (originally TCRTC of Minneapolis, Minnesota, No. 332) are passing at Orange Street. These were two of twenty cars (Nos. 320–339) delivered by St. Louis Car Company to TCRTC between December 1946 and January 1947. They both were part of the thirty cars sold to Public Service Coordinated Transport (PSCT) in March 1953 and were renumbered as noted above. Car No. 10 is now at San Diego. (*Peter D. Ehrlich collection*)

PCC car No. 7 is ready to cross Orange Street in Newark on March 11, 1961. Originally TCRTC car No. 326, this was one of twenty cars (Nos. 320–339) delivered by St. Louis Car Company between December 1946 and January 1947. Each car weighed 37,000 pounds, seated fifty-two passengers, and was powered by four General Electric-type 1220 motors. (*Kenneth C. Springirth photograph*)

On March 11, 1961, PCC car No. 14 (formerly TCRTC car No. 333) is waiting for departure time at Franklin Avenue for the next trip to Penn Station. The TCRTC cars had galvanized steel car bodies and were extra wide cars with a width of 108 inches compared to the 100-inch width of Philadelphia PCC cars. (*Kenneth C. Springirth photograph*)

City Subway car No. 29 (formerly TCRTC car No. 418) is passing near Heller Parkway on March 11, 1961. This was one of five PCC cars (Nos. 415–419) delivered to TCRTC by St. Louis Car Company between June and August 1949. Each car was powered by four General Electric-type 1220 motors. (*Kenneth C. Springirth photograph*)

On March 11, 1961, well-maintained PCC car No. 14 (formerly TCRTC car No. 333) is at Heller Parkway. San Francisco Municipal Railway (SFMR) obtained this car from New Jersey Transit in 2002 for a test to determine the condition of the Newark fleet. In 2004, SFMR purchased eleven ex-Newark PCC cars, including this one. The car was refurbished by Brookville Equipment Corporation, renumbered 1070, and the car exterior was repainted in the Newark, New Jersey, paint scheme of the 1950s. (*Kenneth C. Springirth photograph*)

In this August 31, 1968 scene of PCC car No. 22 (formerly TCRTC car No. 361) crossing Orange Street in Newark, this was the only trolley car street crossing in the entire state of New Jersey at that time. With the later extension of the line, there are now more grade crossings. The car was one of five cars (Nos. 360–364) delivered between July and September 1947 by St. Louis Car Company. Each car was powered by four General Electric-type 1220 motors. (*Kenneth C. Springirth photograph*)

Near Orange Street is the location of this PCC car No. 12 (former TCRTC car No. 331) on August 31, 1968. Orange Street is a street-level station across the road from a bridge across the former electrified Delaware Lackawanna & Western Railroad. (*Kenneth C. Springirth photograph*)

Professionally painted PCC car No. 12 is at the Franklin Avenue terminus of the Newark City Subway on September 1, 1968. Newark has an extensive public transit system, with 39.2 percent of its households without an automobile in 2016 according to the American Community Survey of the U.S. Census Bureau. (*Kenneth C. Springirth photograph*)

On September 1, 1968, PCC car No. 12 is at Franklin Avenue Station waiting for departure time for the next trip to downtown Newark. Built in 1940, this was originally known as the North Sixth Street Newark City Subway Station. With the completion of the turning loop, the station was moved closer to North Fifth Street and renamed Franklin Avenue Station in 1953. (*Kenneth C. Springirth photograph*)

In a new paint scheme, on October 30, 1980, New Jersey Transit PCC car No. 7 is at the Franklin Avenue terminus awaiting departure time. Public Service Coordinated Transport became Transport of New Jersey with the State of New Jersey subsidizing operation on August 23, 1971. The 1978 car requirements were as follows: weekday off peak, five; peak, sixteen; evening, one; Saturday base, four; Saturday evening, one; Sunday base, two; and Sunday evening, one. It became New Jersey Transit when the State of New Jersey took over operation of the City Subway on October 14, 1980. (*Peter D. Ehrlich photograph*)

New Jersey Transit PCC car No. 19 (originally TCRTC No. 338) is leaving the Franklin Avenue Station on October 30, 1986. During 1975, the operable PCC car fleet was painted an attractive red, white, and blue paint scheme. This car was acquired by the San Francisco Municipal Railway in 2004 and restored by the Brookville Equipment Corporation resuming operation in San Francisco in 2011. Renumbered 1078, the car has been painted to honor San Diego Electric Railway, which operated PCC cars from 1937 to 1949 and again in 2011. (*Peter D. Ehrlich photograph*)

Orange Street Station is the location of New Jersey Transit PCC car No. 28 (originally TCRTC car No. 417) on October 30, 1986. During 1985, each car received an additional headlight above the front destination sign to improve lighting for car operators when in the subway. (*Peter D. Ehrlich photograph*)

On July 8, 1997, New Jersey Transit PCC car No. 16 (formerly TCRTC car No. 335) is at the Franklin Avenue Terminus. This was the designated trash trolley car picking up trash at each station. (*Kenneth C. Springirth photograph*)

Heller Parkway Station is a passenger stop for PCC car No. 22 on July 8, 1997. Over the years, Newark's PCC cars have had three paint schemes. The gray original PSTC colors were used until the early 1970s, Bicentennial white with red and blue stripes were used from the early 1970s until 1985, and the black and white with multi-colored stripe was used from 1985 until the last day of PCC car operation on August 24, 2001. (*Kenneth C. Springirth photograph*)

On July 8, 1997, PCC car No. 21 (originally TCRTC car No. 360) is near Orange Street. On February 25, 1953, when PSCT announced it would acquire thirty PCC cars from TCRTC, this was the first car to arrive on August 12, 1953. (*Kenneth C. Springirth photograph*)

Having passed under the Interstate 280 Bridge, Newark City Subway PCC car No. 13 (originally TCRTC car No. 332) is crossing Orange Street for its trip to Newark Penn Station on July 8, 1997. Just north of this bridge is the 360-acre Branch Brook Park. (*Kenneth C. Springirth photograph*)

Passengers are boarding New Jersey Transit PCC car No. 9 (originally TCRTC No. 328) at the Franklin Avenue terminus on July 8, 1997 for the trip to downtown Newark. The Route 7 (City Subway) over the years has provided a first-class PCC car operation in North America. (*Kenneth C. Springirth photograph*)

The operator of PCC car No. 9 took this view of the author, Ken Springirth, alongside car No. 9 at the Newark City Subway Penn Station on July 8, 1997. Located at Raymond Plaza West and Market Street, the current station building was dedicated on March 23, 1935. (*Kenneth C. Springirth collection*)

Route 7 PCC car No. 17 (originally TCRTC No. 336) is crossing Orange Street on July 8, 1997. The Newark City Subway speeded up transit service, which shortened travel time for northern Newark residents and suburban Essex County residents. (*Kenneth C. Springirth photograph*)

On July 8, 1997, PCC car No. 16 is at Heller Parkway Station. On the left side front window, the small sign reads "Work Car," because this is the car that picks up the trash. This station was closed on June 21, 2002 due to its proximity to the Franklin Avenue station. (*Kenneth C. Springirth photograph*)

PCC car No. 22 is near the Franklin Avenue terminus on July 8, 1997. The upper front window screen guard was installed in the 1970s to protect the operator from objects thrown from overhead bridges. This view shows the generally well-maintained Newark City Subway right of way and cars. (*Kenneth C. Springirth photograph*)

On March 5, 1999, New Jersey Transit PCC car No. 12 is at Norfolk Street Station for an outbound trip to Franklin Avenue. This station is located on Norfolk Street just south of Central Avenue in the University Heights neighborhood of Newark. It contained a connection to the Route 23 (Central Avenue) trolley car line until the line was converted to bus operation on December 14, 1947. (*Peter D. Ehrlich photograph*)

PCC car No. 7 is approaching the Franklin Avenue terminal on March 5, 1999. This car entered Newark City Subway service between January and February 1954, and it was used until August 24, 2001. It was in storage at Jersey City, New Jersey, from about 2001 until January 2014. On January 15, 2014, it was acquired by the New York Museum of Transportation in Rush near Rochester, New York. (*Peter D. Ehrlich photograph*)

New Jersey Transit work car No. 5223 is on the Newark City Subway at Franklin Avenue on March 5, 1999. This was originally passenger car No. 2683 that was one of seventy-one double-truck cars (Nos. 2630–2700) built by Public Service Railway Company in 1917. It was converted into work car No. 5223 on July 31, 1953 by Public Service Coordinated Transport. (*Peter D. Ehrlich photograph*)

PCC car No. 21 is approaching Heller Parkway on March 5, 1999. (*Peter D. Ehrlich photograph*)

On October 27, 1999, New Jersey Transit PCC car No. 26 (originally TCRTC car No. 415) is passing car No. 6 (originally TCRTC car No. 325) at Norfolk Street Station. Car No. 6 received a new type of resilient wheels in 1997 to test their operation. It was repainted in 2001 to commemorate the end of PCC car service. It was sold to the Rockhill Trolley Museum via the Friends of the New Jersey Transportation Heritage Center in April 2011. (*Peter D. Ehrlich photograph*)

PCC car No. 20 (originally TCRTC car No. 339) is inbound approaching Davenport Avenue on March 5, 1999. This car was acquired by the San Francisco Municipal Railway in 2004 and was restored in 2011 by Brookville Equipment Corporation, renumbered 1072, and the exterior was repainted in the paint scheme of Servicio de Transportes Eléctricos del Distrito Federal of Mexico City to honor the operation of PCC cars in that city. (*Peter D. Ehrlich photograph*)

With the high-rise apartments in the background that contribute to transit riding for the Newark City Subway, on March 5, 1999, New Jersey Transit PCC car No. 17 is near Heller Parkway. Newark's PCC cars received excellent maintenance over the years, operated on private right of way, and were stored under Penn Station in Newark which contributed to their long-term operation. (*Peter D. Ehrlich photograph*)

On October 27, 1999, Newark City Subway PCC car No. 26 is approaching Davenport Avenue heading for downtown Newark. In this view from the station pedestrian overpass, note the classic wayside signal on the right. (*Peter D. Ehrlich photograph*)

Kinkisharyo car No. 108 has just been delivered to the Grove Street Shop on October 28, 1999. The new three-section, 70 percent low-floor car, designed for a 750-volt DC overhead catenary system, was 26,740 millimeters (87.73 feet) long, 2,680 millimeters (8.79 feet) wide, and 3,630 millimeters (11.91 feet) in height. (*Peter D. Ehrlich photograph*)

Passengers are ready to board arriving Newark City Subway PCC car No. 24 (originally TCRTC car No. 363) at Norfolk Street Station on August 20, 2001. Out of the original thirty-car PCC fleet, cars Nos. 3 and 27 were sold for use on the Shaker Heights routes in Cleveland, Ohio, in 1977. Cars Nos. 8 and 29 were crushed and later scrapped when workers accidentally collapsed part of the Penn Station roof on top of the cars. Car No. 18 was inactive by 1977. Car No. 30 was used for parts and scrapped in 1985. (*Peter D. Ehrlich photograph*)

On August 20, 2001, PCC car No. 12 is at the Branch Brook Park Station located on North Fifth Street Place north of Heller Parkway. This car was acquired by the San Francisco Municipal Railway in 2004 and was restored by Brookville Equipment Corporation, renumbered 1076, and the exterior was repainted in the tropical theme of DC Transit of Washington, D.C. This station, dedicated March 2001 and named for Branch Brook Park, replaced the former Franklin Avenue Station. (*Peter D. Ehrlich photograph*)

PCC car No. 21 is looping at the new Branch Brook Park Station on August 20, 2001. This car was acquired by the San Francisco Municipal Railway in 2004 and was restored in 2011 by Brookville Equipment Corporation, renumbered 1077, and the exterior was repainted in the paint scheme of Birmingham Electric Company, which operated PCC cars from February 15, 1947 until April 19, 1953. (*Peter D. Ehrlich photograph*)

The new Branch Brook Park Station was still under construction as PCC car No. 7 looped around it on August 20, 2001. During 2000, the trolley wire overhead was replaced with a catenary system that required each PCC car to have a pantograph. When New Jersey Transit replaced the PCC cars with the new longer modern Kinkisharyo light rail vehicles, Franklin Avenue Station was closed on August 25, 2001 and replaced by the Branch Brook Park station. (*Peter D. Ehrlich photograph*)

Newark City Subway PCC car No. 1 (originally TCRTC car No. 320) is at the Brook Branch Park Station on August 20, 2001. (*Peter D. Ehrlich photograph*)

Route 7 Newark City Subway PCC car No. 23 (originally TCRTC car No. 362) is approaching the Orange Street Station in Newark on August 20, 2001. This car was acquired by San Francisco Municipal Railway in 2004, was restored by the Brookville Equipment Corporation in 2011, repainted in the bright yellow and forest green color scheme of Twin City Rapid Transit Company of Minneapolis-St. Paul, Minnesota, and renumbered 1071. (*Peter D. Ehrlich photograph*)

Newark City Subway PCC car No. 9 is arriving at Brook Branch Park on August 20, 2001. This car was acquired by San Francisco Municipal Railway in 2004, was restored by the Brookville Equipment Corporation, repainted in the color scheme of Los Angeles Transit Lines (LATL), and renumbered 1080. LATL was taken over in 1958 by the Los Angeles Metropolitan Transit Authority, which converted the system to bus operation. (*Peter D. Ehrlich photograph*)

Branch Brook Park Station is the location of PCC car No. 17 on August 20, 2001. Before arrival of the new cars, the surviving twenty-four PCC cars (Nos. 1-2, 4-7, 9-17, 19-26, and 28) received pantographs in 1999 from the new light rail cars. This made it possible for the rail line to remain in service with PCC cars while the overhead was changed from trolley wire to the catenary system required for pantographs. (*Peter D. Ehrlich photograph*)

On August 20, 2001, outbound New Jersey Transit PCC car No. 15 (originally TCRTC car No. 334) is approaching Bloomfield Avenue Station. This station is located at Bloomfield Avenue on the west side of Branch Brook Park near the park's main entrance. (*Peter D. Ehrlich photograph*)

Inbound PCC car No. 22 is at the Orange Street Station on August 20, 2001. The new overhead contact system has a wire freely suspended called the catenary (mathematical term used to describe the curve in the sagging wire) from which suspenders are attached to the below wire that is contacted by the pantograph on the roof of the light rail vehicle. (*Peter D. Ehrlich photograph*)

In this almost park-like setting, Newark City Subway PCC car No. 7 is gliding into the Davenport Avenue Station on August 20, 2001. The station is located at the dead end of Davenport Avenue east of North 5th Street. (*Peter D. Ehrlich photograph*)

The dense forest of trees around the Davenport Avenue Station on August 20, 2001 provides the setting for Newark City Subway PCC car No. 17. (*Peter D. Ehrlich photograph*)

Inbound PCC car No. 22 is approaching Bloomfield Avenue Station on August 20, 2001. This car was acquired in 2004 by the San Francisco Municipal Railway, restored by Brookville Equipment Corporation in 2011 with repainting in an El Paso 1960s light green with white and red trim paint scheme, and renumbered 1073. El Paso ended streetcar service on September 4, 1974, and it was restored on November 9, 2018. (*Peter D. Ehrlich photograph*)

On August 20, 2001, New Jersey Transit PCC car No. 1 is north of Bloomfield Avenue on a southbound trip to Penn Station in Newark. (*Peter D. Ehrlich photograph*)

On August 20, 2001, outbound New Jersey Transit PCC Car No. 17 is coming into Orange Street Station. This car was acquired in 2004 by the San Francisco Municipal Railway, restored by Brookville Equipment Corporation in 2011 with repainting in the Cleveland Transit System (CTS) color scheme, and renumbered 1075. CTS operated seventy-five PCC cars from 1946 to 1952 when they were sold to the Toronto Transportation Commission. (*Peter D. Ehrlich photograph*)

Branch Brook Park (formerly Franklin Avenue) Station is the location of PCC car No. 1 on August 20, 2001. (*Peter D. Ehrlich photograph*)

Kinkisharyo light rail vehicle No. 109 is outbound approaching Park Avenue Station on August 27, 2001. This station is located in the open cut below the overpass bridge of Park Avenue. (*Peter D. Ehrlich photograph*)

On August 27, 2001, New Jersey Transit Kinkisharyo light rail vehicle No. 114 is on the layup track at Branch Brook Park. (*Peter D. Ehrlich photograph*)

Norfolk Street Station is the location of Kinkisharyo light rail vehicle No. 109 on August 27, 2001. (*Peter D. Ehrlich photograph*)

On a sunny August 27, 2001, outbound Kinkisharyo light rail vehicle No. 111 is leaving Orange Street Station. (*Peter D. Ehrlich photograph*)

On August 27, 2001, Kinkisharyo light rail vehicle No. 111 is coming into the Davenport Avenue Station. (*Peter D. Ehrlich photograph*)

Kinkisharyo light rail vehicle No. 106 is arriving at the Branch Brook Park station on August 27, 2001. (*Peter D. Ehrlich photograph*)

On August 27, 2001, Kinkisharyo light rail vehicle No. 116 is arriving at Branch Brook Park Station. (*Peter D. Ehrlich photograph*)

Leaving Davenport Avenue Station, Kinkisharyo light rail vehicle No. 111 is heading for Newark Penn Station on August 27, 2001. (*Peter D. Ehrlich photograph*)

On August 27, 2001, inbound Kinkisharyo light rail vehicle No. 111 has left Bloomfield Avenue Station. (*Peter D. Ehrlich photograph*)

Outbound New Jersey Transit Kinkisharyo light rail vehicle No. 111 is ready to cross Orange Street on August 27, 2001. (*Peter D. Ehrlich photograph*)

Inbound Kinkisharyo light rail vehicle No. 101 is approaching Bloomfield Avenue Station on August 28, 2001. (*Peter D. Ehrlich photograph*)

On a snowy March 6, 2003, Kinkisharyo light rail vehicle No. 103 is outbound ready to cross Franklin Avenue. (*Peter D. Ehrlich photograph*)

Inbound Kinkisharyo light rail vehicle No. 103 is arriving at Norfolk Street Station on a lightly snow covered March 6, 2003. (*Peter D. Ehrlich photograph*)

On a fresh, snow-covered March 6, 2003, Kinkisharyo light rail vehicle No. 117 is leaving Branch Brook Park Station. New Jersey Transit is the largest statewide public transit system in the U.S., with 260 bus routes, three light rail lines (Hudson-Bergen Light Rail, Newark Light Rail, and River Line), and twelve commuter rail lines. (*Peter D. Ehrlich photograph*)

Kinkisharyo light rail vehicle No. 101 is at Newark Broad Street Station, located on Lackawanna Avenue at University Avenue on August 27, 2001. This is on the Newark Penn Station to Broad Street Station Light Rail Line. It is a commuter rail connection point for the Gladstone Branch (Gladstone via Broad Street to New York), Morristown Branch (Dover via Broad Street to New York), and Montclair-Boonton Line (Hackettstown via Broad Street to New York). (*Peter D. Ehrlich photograph*)

6

Hudson–Bergen Light Rail Line

The Hudson–Bergen Light Rail Line is the first successful transit Design-Build-Operate-Maintain (DBOM) project in the U.S. since World War II. A major benefit of DBOM is that any unwise economy taken by a contractor during the design/build stage of the project will cost that same contractor during the operation phase of the project. Under DBOM, a contractor and owner working together both can do better than if they have an adversarial relationship. The performing contractor needs a major base of in-house engineering development and engineering design capability. Private partners Washington Group and Kinkisharyo formed a special company Twenty First Century Rail Corporation (TFCR) to provide transportation operation including customer service, train dispatch/control center operation, and maintenance of the fixed plant and rolling stock for fifteen years. As noted in the book *Hudson–Bergen Light Rail* by Alfred E. Fazio, P.E.: "Under the terms of the DBOM contract, TFCR's performance is measured by specific parameters which reflect service quality. The most significant of these is the Service Delivery Quality Index (SDQI), an average of On-Time Performance and the number of trains each day which complete their run. The contract defines a target SDQI of 96%; a small bonus is paid to TFCR for any month in which the index exceeds this number, and penalties are assessed against TFCR if the monthly average falls below this target." After bids were received from three teams, New Jersey Transit (NJT) awarded the project to TFCR. The Notice to Proceed was given by NJT to TFCR on November 1, 1996.

Construction began with timber and concrete-filled steel piles to support a new shop building. Active Consolidated Rail Corporation (Conrail) tracks in Bayonne were relocated to the east side of the former Central Railroad of New Jersey right of way. Kinkisharyo began engineering the new light rail vehicle (LRV) based on Kinkisharyo's Type 7 car for Boston and their Dallas car. A 70 percent low-floor car required a double articulated design with three sections supported on three wheel assemblies. Two prototype cars were completed at Kinkisharyo's Osaka, Japan, plant and arrived at Port Newark in January 1999. Kinkisharyo leased a facility in Harrison, New Jersey, where the remaining car bodies and components were shipped and final assembly was completed.

On April 15, 2000, the Hudson–Bergen Light Rail Line (HBLR) opened from Exchange Place to East 34th Street in Bayonne and a branch line to Westside Avenue. Heavy showers and cool temperatures reduced the opening day ridership to an estimated 2,300 to 2,600; however, on July 4, 2000, massive crowds used HBLR to reach Liberty State Park and Exchange Place. HBLR was extended northward to Pavonia–Newport on November 18, 2000. It was extended northward from Pavonia–Newport to NJ Transit's Hoboken Terminal on Sunday September 29, 2002. It reached 22nd Street in Bayonne on November 15, 2003, Lincoln Harbor in Weehawken on September 7, 2004, and Tonnelle Avenue in North Bergen on February 25, 2006. It was completed to its southern terminus at 8th Street in Bayonne on January 31, 2011. In April 2019, the line has three services; Tonnelle Avenue–Hoboken Terminal (weekdays only), West Side Avenue–Tonnelle Avenue, and 8th Street–Hoboken Terminal. HBLR celebrated its sixteenth anniversary in April 2016. It serves high-density commercial and residential areas of Jersey City and Hoboken plus connects to ferries and Port Authority Trans Hudson (PATH), a 13.8-mile rail system that operates four services during the daytime on weekdays: Newark–World Train Center, Hoboken–World Trade Center, Journal Square–33rd Street, and Hoboken–33rd Street. Between 11 p.m. and 6 a.m., Monday to Friday, and all-day Saturday, Sunday, and holidays, PATH operates two train services: Newark–World Trade Center and Journal Square–33rd Street (via Hoboken).

For the 2017 fiscal year (July 1, 2016 to June 30, 2017), HBLR for an average weekday handled 51,939 passengers, average Saturday handled 23,672 passengers, and average Sunday handled 18,878 passengers. This line has fifty-two cars built by Kinkisharyo that are owned by New Jersey Transit and operated via a contract with Twenty First Century Rail. The Hudson River waterfront was in a massive redevelopment because of the high cost of office and home space in Manhattan.

Service intervals according to the April 7, 2018 schedule were as follows: Monday to Friday service intervals were every fifteen to twenty minutes for each of the three lines—Tonnelle Avenue–Hoboken Terminal, West Side Avenue–Tonnelle, and 8th Street–Hoboken Terminal; on Saturday and Sunday, service intervals were every twenty minutes for the two lines running—West Side–Tonnelle Avenue and 8th Street–Hoboken Terminal.

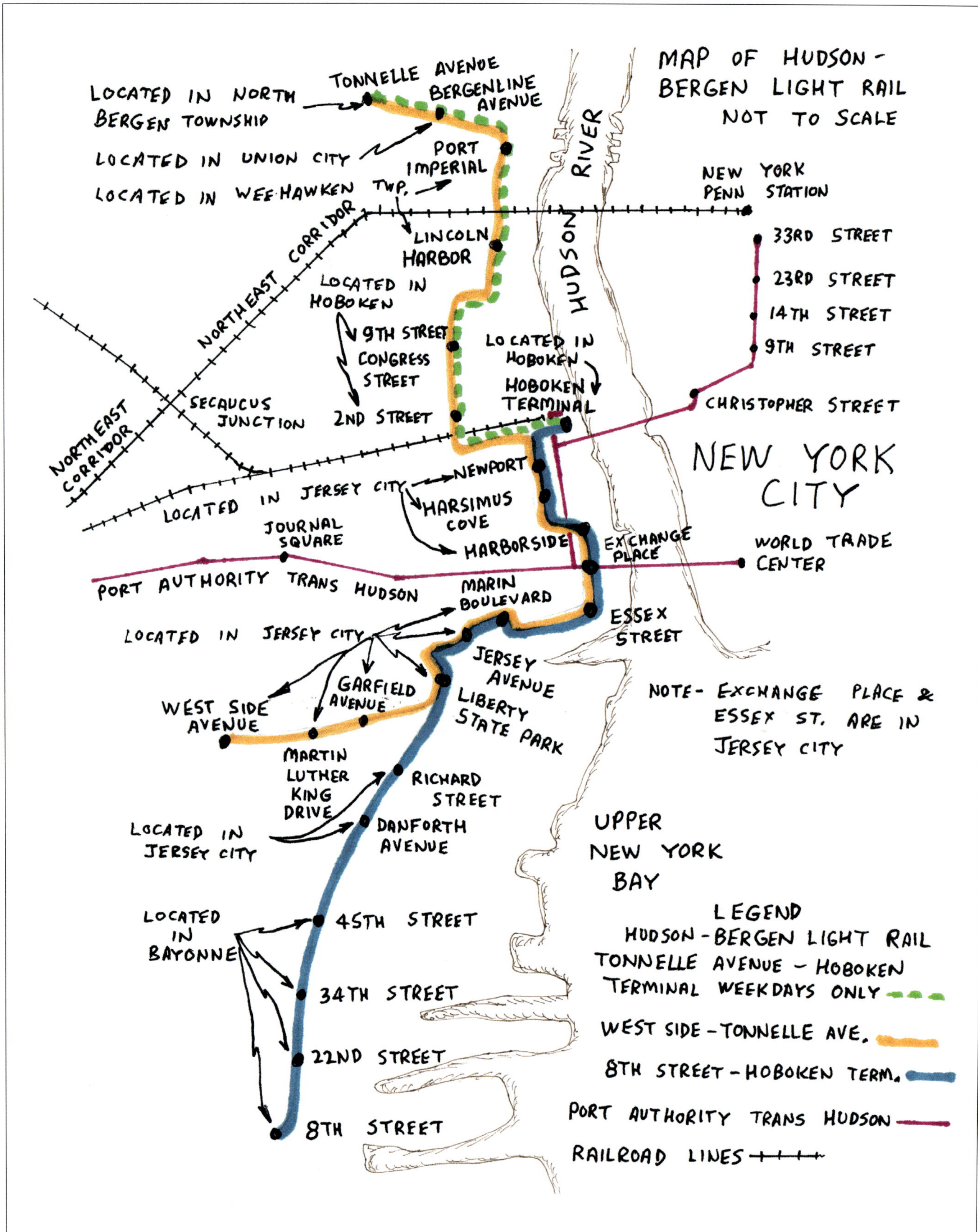

HBLR is a 17-mile system with twenty-four stations that operates from North Bergen Township via Union City Weehawken Township, city of Hoboken, Jersey City, to city of Bayonne, all of which are in Hudson County, New Jersey.

HBLR car No. 2024 is approaching Garfield Avenue station located between Randolph and Garfield Avenues south of Union Street in Jersey City on August 20, 2001. The HBLR car is a 90-foot, high-performance light rail vehicle manufactured by Kinkisharyo Company. It seats sixty-eight passengers with a total capacity of 140, including standees. The HBLR car is designated a 70-percent, low-floor car so that more attractive low floor station platforms could be used. (*Peter D. Ehrlich photograph*)

On August 20, 2001, HBLR car No. 2006 is leaving Martin Luther King Drive Station in Jersey City. Located on the east side of the Martin Luther King Drive, this intersection is protected by Jersey City police officers and traffic lights. About 5,000 daily passengers daily use West Side Branch Stations at Garfield Avenue, Martin Luther King Drive, and West Side Avenue. (*Peter D. Ehrlich photograph*)

On August 28, 2001, HBLR car No. 2005 is outbound at Harborside, an office complex in the Exchange Place district of Jersey City. (*Peter D. Ehrlich photograph*)

HBLR car No. 2006 is at Liberty State Park Station on August 20, 2001. This station is north of the junction of the West Side and Bayonne branch lines and serves as an important transfer point for those two branch lines. Northbound service from this station is available to Hoboken Terminal and Tonnelle Avenue in North Bergen. Southbound service is available to West Side Avenue in Jersey City and 8th Street in Bayonne. (*Peter D. Ehrlich photograph*)

Marin Boulevard Station in Jersey City (located at the foot of Marin Boulevard) is the location of HBLR car No. 2007 on August 20, 2001. (*Peter D. Ehrlich photograph*)

This August 27, 2001 view shows HBLR car No. 2014 at 34th Street Station (a single island station platform near Avenue E) in Bayonne. (*Peter D. Ehrlich photograph*)

HBLR car No. 2004 is approaching Exchange Place Station on March 6, 2003. This station is located on Hudson Street between York and Montgomery Streets in Jersey City. (*Peter D. Ehrlich photograph*)

On March 6, 2003, HBLR car No. 2023 is at the Hoboken Station, which is used by the Hoboken Terminal–Tonnelle Line (weekdays only) and the Hoboken Terminal–8th Street Line. This station is located at the Hudson River waterfront. Nearby are Port Authority Trans Hudson rapid transit system, New Jersey Transit Regional Rail, and buses. (*Peter D. Ehrlich photograph*)

7

River Line

Connecting Camden and Trenton, the 34-mile River Line runs somewhat parallel to the Delaware River. In 1830, this line originally was the Camden–Bordentown section and Bordentown–Trenton Branch of the Camden & Amboy Railroad. The line became part of the Pennsylvania Railroad in 1871. Passenger service was abandoned in 1963. It became Penn Central in 1968, and Conrail from 1976 to June 1, 1999.

In November 1996, New Jersey Transit's board of directors approved light rail transit with diesel light rail transit cars for the Trenton–Camden corridor. Design, Build, Operate, Maintain (DBOM) was chosen, and the notice to proceed was given to Rail Group on December 30, 1999. The diesel trolley River Line began regular service on Sunday March 14, 2004 after a March 13 day of opening ceremonies and VIP runs. The 4-foot 8.5-inch standard gauge line is operated for New Jersey Transit by the Southern New Jersey Rail Group using twenty Stadler diesel light rail units imported from Switzerland.

On May 24, 2004, a fifteen-minute peak headway was introduced. To permit a direct transfer between the River Line and New Jersey Transit's Atlantic City Rail Line, the Pennsauken Transit Center Station opened for passenger service on October 14, 2013.

For the 2017 fiscal year (July 1, 2016 to June 30, 2017), the River Line for an average weekday handled 8,633 passengers, average Saturday handled 5,534 passengers, and average Sunday handled 4,096 passengers. This line has twenty cars owned by New Jersey Transit and operated via a contract with Bombardier Transportation.

River Line service intervals according to the April 17, 2018 schedule was as follows: Monday to Friday peak every fifteen minutes and off peak every thirty minutes; Saturday and Sunday service was every thirty minutes. Daily, the last trip left the Entertainment Center for Trenton around 9 p.m., and the last trip left Trenton for the Entertainment Center around 9 p.m.

Light rail vehicle No. 3517 is at the Entertainment Center Station on Jersey Joe Walcott Boulevard in Camden, which is the River Line's southernmost station, waiting for departure time on May 19, 2019. This is one of twenty Stadler GTW railcars built by Stadler Rail of Switzerland. GTW stands for Gelenktriebwagen, which is an articulated railcar. Street trackage in Camden is 115-pound continuous welded rail embedded in concrete. Just north of the station is a diamond crossover. (*Kenneth C. Springirth photograph*)

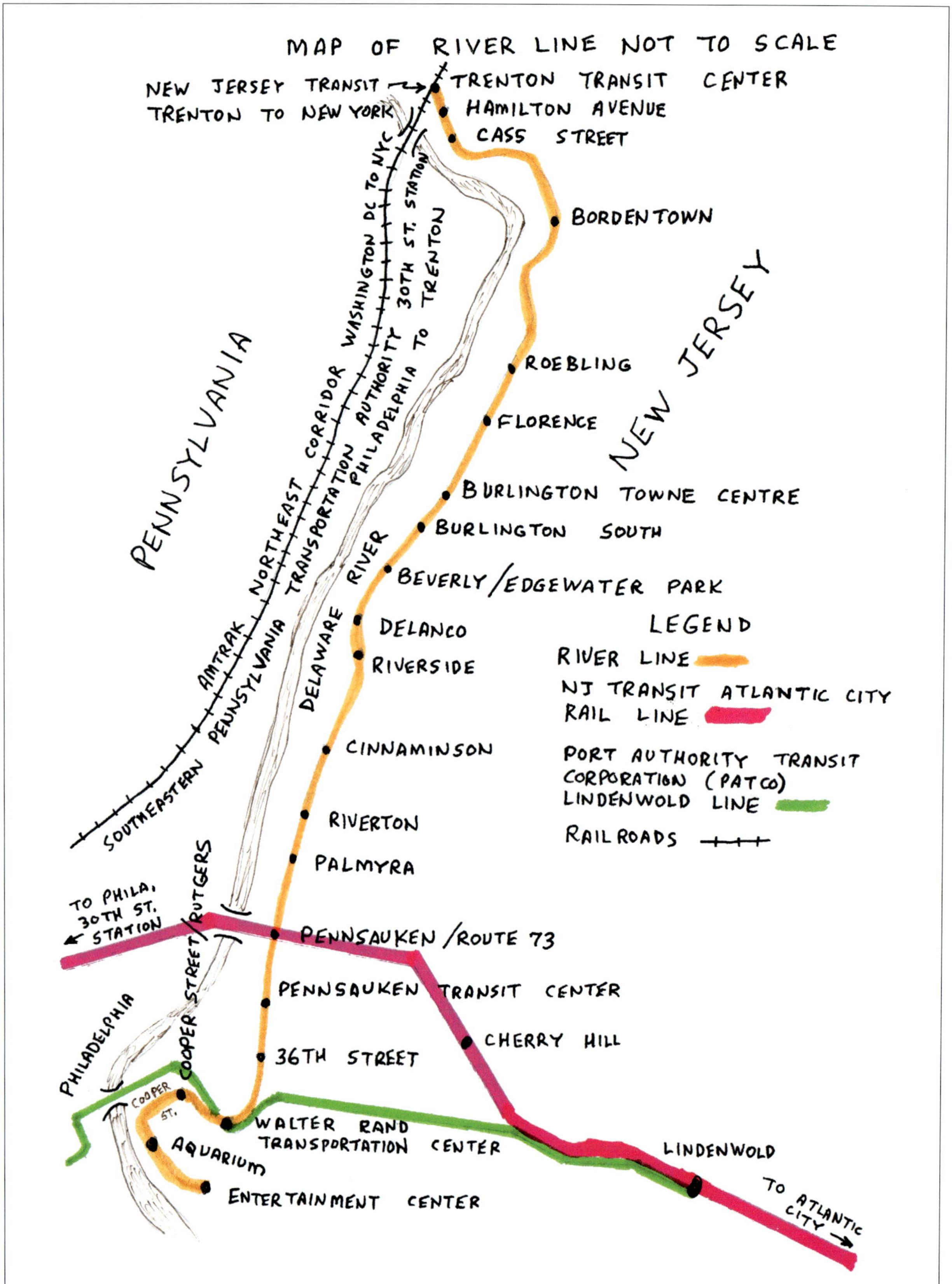

This map of the River Line shows its rail connections at Trenton for Amtrak Northeast Corridor trains, Southeastern Pennsylvania Transportation Authority—Philadelphia to Trenton service—and New Jersey Transit—Trenton to New York service. Pennsauken Station is a connection point for New Jersey Transit—Atlantic City Rail line. Walter Rand Transportation Center is a connection point for Port Authority Transit Corporation (PATCO)—Philadelphia to Lindenwold Line.

Aquarium Station on Delaware Avenue in Camden is the location of River Line two-car train headed by car No. 3514 on May 30, 2004. The 10-foot-wide by 102-foot-long car seats ninety, stands ninety to 100 passengers, and can operate in up to three cars in multiple unit operation. Each car has a short middle "C" section where the diesel engine and generators are located. The "A" and "B" sections each have a full width operator's cab. (*Kenneth C. Springirth photograph*)

The Victor condominium formerly Building 17 of the RCA Victor Camden plant (which originally was a victrola cabinet factory) just north of the Aquarium station in the Cooper Grant neighborhood of Camden is the location of River Line car No. 3517 on May 19, 2019. The Classical Revival building constructed in 1909 by the architectural and engineering firm of Ballinger and Perrot was placed on the National Register of Historic Places on October 4, 2002 and was converted into luxury apartments in August 2003. (*Kenneth C. Springirth photograph*)

On May 30, 2004, River Line car No. 3507 is on Cooper Street in Camden parallel to the tower of the Benjamin Franklin Bridge seen on the right. The River Line links the Waterfront Entertainment District and University District with the Walter Rand Transportation Center where it intersects PATCO's Lindenwold Line enhancing transportation opportunities for both lines. (*Kenneth C. Springirth photograph*)

On March 20, 2004, River Line car No. 3515 is on Cooper Street near the Cooper Street-Rutgers Station serving the nearby Rutgers University Camden Campus, Rowan University Camden Campus, and Camden County College. (*Kenneth C. Springirth photograph*)

Cooper Street near the Cooper Street–Rutgers Station in the Cooper Grant neighborhood of Camden is the location of River Line car No. 3506 (southbound for the Camden Waterfront) on May 19, 2019. On Cooper Street, the southbound platform is west of 2nd Street and the northbound platform for Trenton is east of 2nd Street. Along with the nearby schools of higher education, this station serves as an anchor for the continuing redevelopment of this part of Camden. (*Kenneth C. Springirth photograph*)

The Walter Rand Transportation Center (WRTC) at 100 South Broadway Boulevard in Camden is the location of River Line car No. 3515 on May 30, 2004. This transit center opened on May 17, 1989 as the Camden Transportation Center. It was built above the existing PATCO Broadway Station, which opened as a station on the Philadelphia Rapid Transit Bridge Line on June 7, 1936. That subway line connected 8th and Market in Philadelphia via the Delaware River Bridge and subway to City Hall Station in Camden and terminated at Broadway Station in Camden. In 1953, the Philadelphia Transportation Company opened Locust Street Subway adding stations at 10th, 12th, and 16th Street to the Bridge Line. (*Kenneth C. Springirth photograph*)

Passengers are ready to board River Line car No. 3504 at WRTC on March 20, 2004. WRTC (served by the River Line, Broadway Station of PATCO, New Jersey Transit buses, and Greyhound buses) was named for former New Jersey State Senator Walter Rand (May 31, 1919 to January 6, 1995) who specialized in transportation issues. (*Kenneth C. Springirth photograph*)

A two-car River Line train is crossing the picturesque Rancocas Creek bridge on April 18, 2004. The arch structure provided a higher channel clearance, which eliminated a need for a moveable bridge for this location. Rancocas Creek is a tributary of the Delaware River in southwestern New Jersey. The main part of the creek is 8.3 miles long with a 28.3-mile North Branch and a 21.7-mile South Branch. (*Kenneth C. Springirth photograph*)

Southbound River Line car No. 3518 is passing through Delanco Township in Burlington County, New Jersey, on April 18, 2004. Delanco was named for the Delaware River and Rancocas Creek, which bordered the community. It was originally called Del-Ranco, which was later shortened to Delanco. (*Kenneth C. Springirth photograph*)

On April 18, 2004, northbound River Line car No. 3507 is arriving at the Delanco Station, which is parallel to Pennsylvania Avenue on the north side at Spruce Street and on the south side is Rhawn Street, which leads to Cooper Street. At this location, the 115-pound continuously welded rail is fastened to concrete ties by means of a spring clip assembly. (*Kenneth C. Springirth photograph*)

Beverly/Edgewater Park Station is the location of River Line car No. 3518 on May 30, 2004. This is a single platform station on a single track section of the River Line. (*Kenneth C. Springirth photograph*)

Northbound River Line car No. 3516 is at the Burlington South Station located on W. Broad Street near Keim Boulevard on May 19, 2019. The River Line has a mixture of urban, suburban, and rural scenes. (*Kenneth C. Springirth photograph*)

River Line car No. 3506 is on the single-track ballasted right of way marked by concrete curbs on each side of the tracks in the center of Broad Street at High Street in downtown City of Burlington on May 19, 2019. Fleeing oppression in England, Quakers settled in Burlington in 1677. (*Kenneth C. Springirth photograph*)

On April 18, 2004, River Line car No. 3515 is on Broad at Stacey Street passing by the First Baptist Church of Burlington. The church was organized on December 21, 1800, and the present building was built in 1912. A major fire destroyed much of the church interior in May 1968, and it has been restored. (*Kenneth C. Springirth photograph*)

Northbound River Line car No. 3517 and southbound car No. 3511 are at the Florence Station in Florence Township about 3 miles north of Burlington on May 19, 2019. This is a passing point as much of the River Line is single track requiring on-time operation. Burlink bus Route 5 connects the Florence River Line Station to the Haines Industrial Center. Close to Pennsylvania via the Pennsylvania–New Jersey Turnpike, Florence and nearby towns have become regional warehouse centers. (*Kenneth C. Springirth photograph*)

On March 20, 2004, River Line car No. 3503 is waiting for departure time at the Trenton station, which is the northern terminus of the River Line. Trenton is the state capital of New Jersey, county seat of Mercer County, and briefly served as U.S. capital in November–December 1784. (*Kenneth C. Springirth photograph*)